"Dr. Harris's contributions to American food and culture are immeasurable. With this book, she takes us on an intriguing journey that explores our shared culinary history, and, yes, our braided heritage."

—PADMA LAKSHMI, writer, creator, and host of *Taste the Nation*, and former host and executive producer of *Top Chef*

"Dr. Jessica B. Harris continues to remind us as to why she is the voice of our culture. She teaches us things that are the fabric of who we are, what we eat, and why they're important. With this book, she gives a voice to the inaudible. It should be required reading."

—KWAME ONWUACHI, chef and owner of Tatiana and Dōgon and author of *Notes from a Young Black Chef*

"In *Braided Heritage,* Dr. Harris invites readers to an elegant dinner party of stories, flavors, and history. Through stunning visuals and the voices of cultural stewards like Sean Sherman, Kit Bennett, Leni Sorensen, and others, Dr. Harris explores how Native, European, and African American traditions intertwine to shape our nation's culinary legacy. With her signature warmth and insight, she celebrates the complexity, richness, and diversity of America's food culture—ultimately taking a seat at the table herself as our omnivorous curator."

—CARLA HALL, chef, author, Emmy Award–winning TV personality, and host of *Chasing Flavor*

BRAIDED HERITAGE

JESSICA B. HARRIS

BRAIDED HERITAGE

RECIPES AND STORIES ON THE ORIGIN OF AMERICAN CUISINE

PHOTOGRAPHS BY KELLY MARSHALL

CLARKSON POTTER/PUBLISHERS

NEW YORK

To good friends.
Good friends I've had.
Good friends I've lost along the way.
So, this is for the old friends sadly lost,
the new friends mercifully still coming,
and the steadfast crew of ever-constant stalwarts.
You know who you are, and more importantly,
I know who you were and who you are.
My heartfelt and abundant thanks to you all.

CONTENTS

THREE IS A MAGIC NUMBER

ESTABLISHING THE AMERICAN BRAID

What is America? The name itself is contentious, taken from an Italian explorer and used to define two continents that were already occupied by whole civilizations. In the United States, we consider ourselves Americans, but Canadians, Mexicans, and Brazilians are also "Americans" in the original sense. The politics of the past years have told us that the United States are anything but united. So, in penning an American cookbook, I ask: How to define the country of my birth? In the 1950s when I went to school, it would have been much simpler, in a sense, as I would have hewed to the then-textbook definition that spoke of Columbus, Washington, Founding Fathers, and Indians. Back then, the white cowboys were contrasted with brown Indians, who spoke like Tonto (think of that name!) and were called things like Princess Summer Fall Winter Spring. African Americans, if considered at all, were graciously accorded George Washington Carver and Booker T. Washington, and enslavement was glossed over in images of white-pillared houses and cotton fields. We have come far, even though there is much more road to travel. The question remains, and in fuller terms: How to define the foundational cultures of this diverse, dynamic, and difficult-to-parse country?

As I pondered this question, I remembered years ago there was a Saturday morning television cartoon show called *Schoolhouse Rock!* The show taught grammar and eventually civics and mathematics. They had songs that served as devices with which to initiate the teaching process. My favorite was, "Three Is a Magic Number."

Three is *indeed* a magic number. It is the number that the Yoruba people of southwestern Nigeria attribute to the trickster orisha, Elegba (Ellegua or Ellegbara), the deified ancestor and owner of the crossroads who has been known to deceive the unsuspecting. Three is an important number in the Christian church: Father, Son, and Holy Ghost. Even in matters culinary there are references made to varying Holy Trinities of seasonings and spices. The more I thought, the more I realized that three is also a magic number when referring to the United States and its history.

The early, original foodways of this country are the result of an intricate braiding of three overarching cultures: Native American, European, African. The result, as we all know, is savory and varied indeed. Each brought much to the bubbling cauldron of cultures that would spawn the nation's food. Native peoples maintained traditions of innovative agriculture as well as highly developed skills in hunting and foraging. Europeans brought the nascent culinary impulses that would form the national cuisines of the four colonizing countries: Spain, Britain, the Netherlands, and France. The Europeans are also the people responsible, in a sense, for the third strand in the braid: They enslaved the Africans, who came with agricultural knowledge and skills in animal husbandry and in growing key foods, as well as their own culinary techniques.

I am well aware, I should note, that when I speak of three cultures in terms of generic Native Americans, Europeans, and Africans, I am committing a grievous fault because each of those overarching cultures has multiple unique subdivisions and each of those has its own specificities, history, culture, foodways, and more. But as on the African continent, there can be some general ideas drawn from the differing culinary cultures of the Asante and the Yoruba, the Kikuyu, the Fon, the Wolof, Khoi, and more. The same, in general, can be said for differences among the British, the French, the Spanish, and the Dutch of the time, and of the distinctions between the Cherokee, and Miwok, the Wampanoag, the Shinnecock, and the Paiute, to name a few. However, the vastness of the part of the North American continent that would become today's United States of America, the broad nature of the general topic, and a general oh-so-United States-ian ignorance of history unfortunately, lends itself all too well to generality.

Perhaps, though, that can be a good thing, in that it forces a look back at former assumptions, and a look at the very nature and fluidity of history. A few reorienting suggestions should suffice. (This is a cookbook, after all.)

Let's begin by resetting the notion of history. It is now generally accepted that Paleo-Indians crossed the land bridge over the Bering Strait onto the continent that would be named North America considerably more than fifteen thousand years ago. They were the first humans to arrive on the land mass that would become the United States, and they made it theirs. They settled homelands, established trade routes, and created myriad cultures, many of which endure until this day. In general compass, their religious traditions did not support the notion of ownership of land, but instead placed the accent on community and continuity. The sacredness of land—and what grew and roamed on it—was an almost universal concept among these societies. The land was there for all, and its bounty was a blessing that was bestowed upon the people. Farming practices were established, hunting grounds were decided, culinary traditions were formed. All of these were well developed long, long before the Europeans set foot on the continent.

Up until recently, those traditions were rarely counted in the American narrative. In 1974, culinary historian Evan Jones entitled the first chapter in his book *American Food: The Gastronomic Story,* "Puritans and Plantations," as if American food started with the Pilgrims. That book—and that common perspective, indeed the one taught to me in my childhood history classes— further flattens the story by telling it solely from the British point of view, beginning with the Jamestown settlement and the landing on Plymouth Rock.

It was never mentioned that years before Sir Walter Raleigh tried to settle the lost colony of Roanoke in 1590, before Jamestown was established in Virginia in 1607, and long before the Pilgrims landed in 1620, the Spanish had already established the city of Saint Augustine in Florida in 1565. The Dutch were also here and had established New Netherland in the area that would become New York in 1614—after Jamestown, but before Plymouth. The French were relatively late into what would become the United States; they initially came as trappers and explorers and arrived in large numbers in the seventeenth and eighteenth centuries. Still their relationships with the other two original American groups—Native Americans and African Americans—were rarely if ever mentioned in those history lessons, and were certainly complex.

Similarly, it has already been written that the first Africans arrived in Jamestown in 1619, a year before the *Mayflower*, but those enslaved Africans were not the first on this land; they were merely the first ones arriving in the British colonies. There were already Africans, and their descendants, in the Spanish colonies with records showing that there were fifty-six enslaved in Saint Augustine in 1602. By 1626 there were also enslaved Africans living in Dutch New Netherland, who made up a sizeable portion of the community. The French had a different relationship with enslavement. Early on, they enslaved large numbers of Indigenous people, many of whom were vanquished members of rival tribes gifted to them as tribute by Natives. However, by the mid-nineteenth century, those enslaved by the French were in large majority Africans and their descendants.

By the year 1776, the place that would become the United States of America was not just about Pilgrims and plantations, but was an increasingly rich mixture of Native Americans from large swaths of the Eastern seaboard, multiple European communities of different classes, and Africans from western and central parts of that continent eating foods as diverse as corn pone, okra soup, and bean pottage. And we begin to see those foods come together.

This then is the American braid. Acknowledging the existence of many hands and many cultures and many ways of growing, hunting, fishing, and foraging and cooking, serving, and eating of necessity, changes the picture of the formation of the American pot.

An oft-quoted proverb asserts that, until the lion speaks, tales of the hunt shall always glorify the hunter. That is indeed the case in modern times. Imagine world history if it were written by the vanquished, not the victors; the underlings, not the overlords. Or, if both were put together, then there might be an equity of experience.

In this book, I have attempted to give diverse—it would be folly to claim "all"— parts of the American braid a voice. In the beginning, I consulted histories and old texts to paint a picture of these foodways as they likely existed in the first decades and centuries after contact between the Native peoples, the Europeans, and the Africans. But in thinking of what recipes to include in this book, I kept coming back to the fact that the story of food is always personal; recipes that are "traditional" are inevitably cooked differently in one family versus the next, and dishes evolve in these hands, from one generation to the next, or perhaps from one meal to the next. I have been a culinary historian for many decades, but I have been a person devoted to the pleasures of sharing conversation around the table for far longer.

Realizing that I had friends both of long standing and recently made from each thread of the braid, I went to them and asked them for tales and recipes from their own tables that reflected their cultures, that spoke to them of their family's and community's past. It was a deeply personal and revealing journey with each friend reflecting on family and food, personal history, and memory. A New Orleans friend revealed himself to be a direct descendant of the first surviving male child born in the French colonies—that is, the first established French family on this land. He offered me not only recipes from his family, but also one from an African American family cook who might have been enslaved. A Native American friend rhapsodized about the strawberry shortcake that was a hallmark of her Shinnecock tribe's Spring Meeting. An African American friend whose family had never seen the South offered thoughts of salmon cooked in milk and sardine sandwiches on white bread, while a white Charleston friend whose last name evokes rice mills and stately plantation houses stated boldly and categorically that in her childhood household, the food that was eaten was African because of the African American cooks who worked there. The conversations and the recipes elicited revealed that the American braid begins early and runs deep. We are all affected by the food and traditions of others.

I have gathered the stories, and family and community recipes of these friends, the ones that point to their past and perhaps to the origin point of American cuisine. I have added my own, too—dishes that represent the roots of my own African American family and my personal experience to widen the lens. And through these recipes, I hope to tell a larger story of how our past was formed, and how that past refracts into our present. Of course, outside the scope of this work are the infinite contributions of those who have come to this land after this first commingling of the three strands of the braid—the mighty waves of immigrants of the past two and a half centuries, who brought such culinary icons as the hamburger, the hot dog, the pizza, to say nothing of tacos, wontons, sushi, and soup joumou.

Our American food, perhaps more than any other aspect of our contentious conjoined cultures, shows us who we are at heart (not to say at stomach!). This American cookbook is not a work of history, but rather an attempt to remind us of just how magnificently mixed we are on the plate, and have been from the very beginning of our national story.

THE NATIVE

PEOPLES

In the beginning, they were here! It's as simple as that. Call them Native Americans, Indigenous Peoples, First Peoples, or as does the Smithsonian Museum on the Mall in DC, American Indians. Whatever denomination you wish to use, the fact remains that they were here First: before the Europeans, before the Africans. Attempting to date their arrival time on this continent is complicated. Recent research using DNA testing, and being mindful of the oral traditions of the Native peoples, suggest that that there may have been a Native American presence in this hemisphere more than 36,000 years ago. Other scholars, in what some feel is a highly controversial move, suggest moving the line back to 130,000 plus years ago. Clearly, we aren't sure. The fact remains that in the beginning of our nation's story, they were here, and they had been a long-established presence when first contact with arriving Europeans occurred.

The names of the peoples are many, and the fact that many of these names are not broadly known speaks to the destruction and devastation caused by contact: Wampanoag, Pequot, Narragansett, Mohegan, Shinnecock, Mohawk, Seneca, Shawnee, Creek, Cherokee, Choctaw, Chickasaw, Seminole, Tunica, Biloxi, Comanche, Arapaho, Wichita, Cheyenne, Diné, Apache, Zuni, Hopi, Pueblo, Bella Bella, Chinook, Haida, Nootka, Paiute, Nez Perce, Serrano, Miwok, Pomo, Shasta, Yokuts, and more—so many, many more.

They lived across a wide range of climates and ecosystems, and had diets that reflected their regions, with as much variety as evidenced in the difference between, for example, the food of the British and that of the Sicilians.

Those in coastal regions depended on the bounty of the Atlantic and Pacific oceans and had diets that were rich in a variety of fish. In the Northeast, there was lobster. Anyone sitting down to a $70 lobster dinner today would be amazed by the lobsters then, left to grow old and to a size that must have looked like prehistoric monsters. They were so abundant that they were used as everyday fare, as fertilizer, and as bait with which to catch the more-desirable cod. There was also an abundance of mollusks: mussels, clams, oysters, and more. Thomas Hariot, an English ethnographer, astronomer, and linguist who documented the failed Roanoke expedition, looked into the waters of the North Carolina Outer Banks and recognized sturgeon, herring, trout, alewife, and mullet in abundance. He might not have had to look too far down because, as Captain John Smith reported in 1608 in Virginia, he saw a massive school of fish "Lying so thicke with their heads above the water" that his boat could scarcely get through. Indeed, from February to May, the Algonquians who lived in the area were dependent on the sea and the bounty it yielded. It all seemed nothing short of miraculous to the Europeans who arrived. The Native peoples fished, sun-dried, and smoked fish and shellfish on racks of branches as depicted by Englishman John White in his 1590 illustrations. Salmon marked the Northwest with the same abundance.

Game was also varied, and available in prodigious quantities. Having been on Martha's Vineyard when the deer are in rut, I can easily understand why venison was the major animal protein in the Northeast, and indeed in much of the country. Hunting was very serious business indeed, with methods developed and perfected to stalk game. In the Southeast, Choctaw and Chickasaw were recorded as using animal skins as methods of disguise, with an astounding level of nuanced skill and mastery. As reported in Dumont du Montigny's 1753 *Mémoires Historiques sur la Louisiane*:

When a deer was killed, the hunter first cut off the head as far down as the shoulders.

> *. . . then he skins the neck without cutting the skin and having removed the bones and flesh from it, he draws out all the brains from the head. After this operation, he replaces the bones of the neck very neatly and fixes them in place with the aid of a wooden hoop and some little sticks. . . . He carries it with him hung to his belt when he goes hunting, and as soon as he perceives a bison or deer, he passes his right hand into the neck of this deer, with which he conceals his face, and begins to make the same kind of movements the living animal would make.*

On the Plains, the buffalo indeed roamed in such numbers and their herds were so vast that the pounding of their hoofs sounded like thunder. When they were hunted and butchered, the uppermost layers of fat and meat were often transformed into pemmican by pounding it with the wild berries that were regularly available and consumed; this preserved both items, and provided a portable, calorie-dense food with a range of nutrients. While buffalo meat was the food mainstay on the Plains, other animals like bear, antelope, and occasionally smaller game were also eaten.

Throughout much of the land, corn was so important that it was, and is, considered a primordial mother by many groups. The growing of corn was often part of an elegantly designed system of agriculture that we know in the Anglo world as the Iroquoian Triad, or the Three Sisters. In it, corn, beans, and squash are planted together to grow in symbiotic harmony. The beans use the corn stalks for support and the squash leaves shade the young plants. The result is a more abundant harvest and, when eaten together, the three foods provide a complete protein.

While tribal social and political structures varied, groups of tribes often banded together to form powerful alliances, the largest of which was known to Europeans as the Haudenosaunee Confederacy. It comprised members of the Cayuga, Mohawk, Oneida, Onondaga, and Seneca who came together to aid each other through trading and mutual support, even sharing food in times of war and famine. It has been argued that some aspects of their representative form of governance may have been folded into the ideas of the original framers of the American constitution.

Their tradition of mutual aid was perhaps at the basis of the help that was offered to the initial European settlers, like the bushels of corn that the Oneida sent to George Washington during the Revolutionary War.

While the Native peoples' world was not entirely the romanticized Peaceable Kingdom, it was nonetheless a world of interdependency and self-sufficiency that would be disrupted and devastated after contact with the Europeans. The Wampanoag and Shinnecock met the British in the coastal Northeast; the Natchez, the Biloxi, and others met the French and the Spanish in the Southeast; the Sioux, Iowa, and Plains Cree met the French in the headwaters of the Mississippi and Missouri rivers, while others met the Spanish downriver. Contact with Europeans settlers, trappers, and conquistadors was not a happy time for any of them.

Despite destruction and privation, some of their descendants continue their foodways, whether through preservation of traditional ingredients and techniques, or through replication, evolution, or reimagination, wherever they are.

Julianne Vanderhoop, a Wampanoag chef from the island of Martha's Vineyard, cooks a contemporary version of her tribe's seafood-rich traditional foods, while Sean Sherman, an Oglala Lakota chef, focuses on researching and developing a decolonized cuisine: imagining what indigenous foods would look like today had colonialism never reached this land. Renée Hunter, a Shinnecock whose father lived on the reservation on eastern Long Island until his death at 104, still craves the tastes of dishes from her childhood summer visits and continues some of the tribe's culinary traditions in her Manhattan apartment.

The American braid begins, by necessity, with the Indigenous peoples. John Barbry, a Tunica-Biloxi, probably expressed it best when he simply stated that, "the Tunica and the Biloxi encountered the French in 1699. So, we've had that relationship for a long time. Of course, we would be influenced by French culture and the people. . . . It's hard to kind of break those things apart."

Through the course of post-contact history, new grains, fruits and vegetables, and meats have been added to traditional diets for most Native communities, for good and for otherwise. The fry bread that many associate with the foods of the Southwest speaks more to the wheat flour and the cooking traditions of Europeans—and yes, colonialism—than to the original traditions of the Native peoples; fry bread is itself an object with two stories: one, of oppression and the forced replacement of Native foods, another, of resilience and resourcefulness in the face of that oppression.

Among many Native peoples, though, there is a growing movement to decolonize food and return to the traditional ways of eating and to traditional forms of food production, where plants were grown in symbiotic harmony with the land. Their work posits hope for the future and a return to more agri-culture, and less agri-business.

MOSHUP'S CHILD

JULIANNE VANDERHOOP

I no longer remember when I first met Juli Vanderhoop; I knew her great-uncle and vividly remember the taste of his simple but delicious food served at his café on the cliffs of what was then called Gay Head on the Massachusetts island of Martha's Vineyard. African Americans have been summer residents of the island for more than a century and a half. My parents were among the families who bought summer houses there, and I have returned to it every year since, making it a place to which I have a deep connection of over half a century.

The Native origin story, though, stretches much farther back: The Wampanoag story tells of Moshup, the giant who shaped the land of Noepe, now called Martha's Vineyard. He was responsible for the glorious multihued cliffs of Gay Head, an area that is today again called Aquinnah, after its Wampanoag name, and meaning "land under the hill." Anyone driving on their way to those cliffs seeing Julianne Vanderhoop scurrying around the Orange Peel Bakery might assume she was just another of the many summer workers on this famed island off the coast of Massachusetts. But if they happen to see her a few hours later, as she curates her offerings of bread, pies, local honey, house-made granolas, and drinks, or prepping her menu

of Thursday night pizzas and full suppers on Sundays, cooked in the beehive stone oven that she had painstakingly constructed, they might think, "Wow, that's an enterprising individual!" They would only begin to get the real measure of Julianne.

Juli, as she is known to all's fiefdom, is situated on the road to the Aquinnah Cliffs and surrounded by forest lands, where dappled sunlight plays off the small brook that runs through it. Her bakery is on her family land near Black Brook; it is land that is sacred to the Wampanoag tribe.

Juli comes by her enterprise and her commitment naturally. The Vanderhoop family is legendary on the island. Juli's relative, Napoleon Madison, wearing full tribal regalia, appeared on the postcards of my youth. He was the medicine man of the Aquinnah Wampanoag tribe. Juli's brother Buddy is a renowned fishing charter boat owner who has taken out such island notables as James Taylor, Jim Belushi, President Obama, and Spike Lee. Her grandfather used to play with Tashtego, the legendary whaler, and her great-uncle Amos Smalley killed the whale that was immortalized as Moby Dick.

The Native peoples are a quiet presence on the island that has become known as a vacation spot for the rich and famous. Aquinnah is the smallest of its townships, with a population of 439 in the 2020 census. Forested thickets contrast with the dunes and crashing Atlantic waves on the beaches of the island's south shore, and the awe-inspiring splendor of the multicolored clay cliffs. The township is a throwback to days long gone.

Juli herself, though, is an oh-so-modern woman who has done everything from working as an early childhood educator to piloting commercial jets. When she returned to her native Aquinnah after years in "America"—as the mainland is called by many on the island—she rapidly became active in the town's life. She is currently on several island boards and is a select person of the town and active in its governance.

It's not surprising, then, that when Juli set her sights on working in food, she became a culinary force in her "up-island" location. She had been taught to bake by her stepfather, Luther Madison. Baking had been a type of meditation for him, as she once told an interviewer for *Edible Vineyard*:

> They told him he had two months to live, but he'd make pies every day and lived for 16 more years. When he wasn't feeling well, he'd roll out of bed and make the crust. Then go back to bed. Then he'd get up to fill the pies. Then back to bed. Then up to put the lid on. Back to bed. Up to bake the pies. Back to bed. It was his meditation. Watching this process, I fell in love with food and the oven.

To me, she mused:

> Although my heritage is mixed, I was raised Native, a lifelong [tribal] member here on the island. I guess Natives these days would say, "It's not about your blood quantity, it's about your system of values." I feel that being born and raised on our territorial homeland definitely has helped me to grasp the real meaning of the community and what our environment brings into our lives. . . . Where I was raised, you are challenged every day by

the weather that was around you or things like that. You really had to find a balance to get through the day and that's what was impressed upon me from a young child, that the Gay Headers were strong and that they had the will to survive and get things done. That's what I was taught.

The natural world of Aquinnah/Gay Head was always a constant in Juli's life.

> I was really raised out on the dunes. The earth yielded its bounty. In the summertime, we'd have plenty of fish, plenty of bass. The fish would change in the wintertime as we went onto the boats. So we would have a lobster, flounder, and monkfish if we were kind of lucky. (Even though monkfish wasn't eaten really a lot back then! It was called goosefish. We'd more play with it on the beach, and my father would warn us about its jaws.)
>
> Sometimes, I would go watch my father fishing. I would collect everything from steamers to mussels and what we called sweetmeats—I don't even know the real name for them! There were always quahogs; there were always lobsters. I've always loved raw shellfish and I love to go shellfishing. We'd go down and we'd do the wiggle waggle with our feet; we dance around and pull at least 40 or 50 clams. Then we'll go home. We'll cook some and we'll have some on the half shell and it's definitely a great experience.
>
> There was also venison, as well as ducks and geese. My grandfather had a big garden, but our vegetables, honestly, I don't remember at all. There were cranberries and we even have a holiday in honor of the cranberry. Aquinnah wasn't such a bad place for a kid.

Juli is very much a person of her place, and her community is of primary importance to her. It is so important, that during her global travels as a pilot, she eventually decided to come back home to this small island. When she returned in the early 2000s, she was looking for something to do. A friend suggested that as she was thinking of working in the food realm and loved baking she start a bakery. She imported a wood-burning beehive oven and built it by hand. That oven now serves as an anchor for the community. Owned by a Native person wanting to fill a seat at the culinary table on Martha's Vineyard, in the space that is her ancestral homeland, her Orange Peel Bakery welcomes not only summer visitors, but especially year-round residents of Aquinnah and members of the community. They come to eat, buy baked goods, catch up on local news, or purchase food they may not be able to get nearby, miles from the nearest supermarket or grocery store. The bakery, with its large yard, festively decorated with lights and charming mismatched furniture, is a gathering place as much as it is a business. (In fact, the baked goods are offered with a box by the door for your cash—on an honor system.)

Juli's oven has multiple purposes. Aside from the delicious breads and cookies that she bakes and offers for sale at her bakery, she uses the oven to create community. Aquinnah is the smallest and the poorest of the towns on the Vineyard, with little year-round commerce, and its up-island location can make it feel remote and distanced from the other towns on the island. But, with events like Pizza Night, a weekly happening that has been going on for more than a decade, Juli brings together not only tribal members and locals but also tourists and down-islanders, and, as her reputation grows in the culinary world, food lovers from all over. She provides the pizza base; guests have to bring their own toppings. The pizzas are expertly baked and then served to those who brought the ingredients. In recent years, Juli has gone beyond Pizza Night and now hosts catered dinners, concerts, and pop-ups featuring chefs of color from around the world, where the food is all prepared in that huge oven. Or she may do a menu featuring the fish and shellfish that

have long sustained the Wampanoag, that she remembers so fondly from her youth. Sitting around the outdoor tables near the oven on any given summer afternoon, it is heartening to notice the number of folks from both within and without the immediate Aquinnah community who stop to pick up goods or just to say hi. Juli has used food to provide an anchor for her community and has shared her community's way with food and life with the world.

The bakery is also a place that Juli has developed into a year-round business: no mean feat in a very small spot on a seasonal island. During COVID, the bakery became a community hub offering foods that residents might otherwise have had to drive about twenty miles down-island to obtain. There are also a growing number of Orange Peel branded items and a book exchange brimming with books donated by and of interest to the community. The bakery has not only allowed her to earn a living, it has cemented her community together.

The other part of Juli's community work is about embracing the traditional crafts and contemporary culture of her people. She keeps bees, selling and using their honey, and is creating a line of products that will take her traditional foods beyond the immediate community. Juli has steadily moved beyond her Aquinnah surroundings to bring the word of her cooking and Wampanoag traditions to others both down-island at events like the Martha's Vineyard African American Film Festival and the Martha's Vineyard Museum's first food symposium, but also beyond the Vineyard community in articles in local and national newspapers and on television shows as well. Her efforts were honored by her 2023 receipt of the Vineyard's prestigious Martha's Vineyard Community Foundation's Creative Living Award.

Her recipes celebrate the Wampanoags' connections to the sea, and to the land on which she lives, the island that they called Noepe.

SUGAR MAPLE

The sugar maple, a tree in the lychee family, is native to eastern Canada and the eastern United States, best known for producing the maple sugar and maple syrup that top today's pancakes and were a vital sweetener in Native cuisines for centuries.

The Abenaki have lived in what became northeastern Vermont for thousands of years, and have long been cultivating sugar maple trees and producing syrup on their land using traditional methods to tap the sap. The sap, a clear liquid, is collected in springtime and boiled to concentrate the sugar. The leaves, which have their own sweetness, are also eaten, as are the inner bark and seeds.

Like the Abenaki, the Ojibwe of Minnesota also harvested maple sugar. To harvest the sugar, a hole is bored into the tree, a spigot is pushed into the hole, and the spigot diverts the sap into a collection container. Finally, the collected sap is put into a large kettle and boiled. The Ojibwe people boiled the sugar down to granules that became their primary seasoning. Other groups created syrups; both were valued as trading goods. Historically, women played a major role in sugar production, but with the need for wood cutters, water gatherers, and more, there was work for everyone and sugar making became a time of coming together.

CRANBERRIES AND CRANBERRY DAY

Cranberry bushes are low vines of small evergreen shrubs that grow in sandy soil of the northern hemisphere; anyone driving along the lower Cape Cod highways can peer out the car window at cranberry bogs. In commercial cultivation, the bogs are flooded in autumn for harvest, which ideally takes place after the first frost. In recent decades, cranberries have been recognized as a superfood, and are now touted as being able to prevent urinary tract infections, reduce inflammation, improve heart health, reduce cavities, and maintain digestive health.

The fruit, twenty-first century virtues notwithstanding, is a traditional one for the Wampanoag tribe, who do not flood them, but let them grow naturally. On the second Tuesday in October, members of the Wampanoag tribe of Aquinnah on Noepe, as the island of Martha's Vineyard is known to them, celebrate Cranberry Day. The bogs and vines have been tended on Noepe for over two hundred years, owned by the tribe as part of their trust land.

On Cranberry Day, tribal children are excused from school, relatives arrive, and food is prepared for the communal supper that will end the day. The food may include clam fritters, clear broth clam chowder, and stuffed quahogs, all traditional dishes. And there are always many forms of cranberries celebrating the age-old connection of the simple North American berry with the People of the First Light.

BEER-BATTERED MAPLE LEAVES
AND CRANBERRY SYRUP

SERVES 6 TO 8

Sugar maple trees are abundant in the Northeast, and maple was the traditional sweetener for many of the Native peoples. The syrup and sugar of maple are vital, but the leaves of the tree are also edible, slightly sweet in taste, and make a surprising snack when battered and fried. While Juli developed the recipe on her own, it is interesting to note that sugar maple leaves are also fried in tempura batter and eaten in Japan. Sugar maple leaves are worth the effort to find. The young leaves that can be foraged in the spring are surprisingly tasty.

Here, the fritters are served with a syrup that Juli devised that combines the sweetness of maple sugar and the bracing tartness of the cranberries that were a major foodstuff and source of vitamins for the Wampanoag.

Vegetable oil, for frying
2 cups all-purpose flour
2 teaspoons baking powder
½ cup dark beer
15 to 20 medium-sized maple leaves
Powdered sugar, for sprinkling
Cranberry Syrup (recipe follows) or maple syrup, for serving

1. Pour 1½ inches of oil into a Dutch oven and heat over medium heat to 350°F. Line a baking sheet with paper towels and set near the stove.

2. In a medium bowl, mix the flour and baking powder together and gently stir in the beer, leaving a splash or two behind, until the batter comes together. The batter should coat the back of a spoon but not be loose and runny; if it's too thick, add the rest of the beer. Do not overmix the batter; just get it mostly smooth.

3. Working in batches, dip the leaves one at a time into the batter and immediately place in the oil to fry until golden brown, about 90 seconds. Flip and fry about 90 seconds more. Place the leaves on the paper towels.

4. Sprinkle them with powdered sugar before serving with cranberry or maple syrup.

CRANBERRY SYRUP
MAKES ABOUT 2¼ CUPS

Cranberry syrup can be used in cocktails, such as mimosas, or added to seltzer to make a refreshing summertime swig!

1 pound cranberries, fresh or frozen
1½ cups maple syrup
1½ tablespoons fresh lemon juice

1. In a heavy pot, combine the cranberries, syrup, and 1½ cups water and bring to a boil over high heat. Reduce the heat to medium and simmer briskly until the consistency is slightly thicker than water, about 45 minutes.

2. Remove from the heat and use a potato masher to crush the berries to a slightly chunky consistency. (Alternatively, transfer to a blender and pulse 10 to 20 times.)

3. Transfer to a fine-mesh sieve set over a medium bowl and strain, pressing on the solids gently to extract the liquid. Discard the solids.

4. Add the lemon juice and allow to cool to room temperature before transferring to a container. Store in the refrigerator for up to 10 days or in the freezer for up to 1 month.

CLEAR BROTH CLAM CHOWDER

SERVES 6 TO 8

The word "chowder" may come from the French term *chaudron* or *chaudière,* meaning "a cauldron," but the main ingredients of this dish are the clams that were the culinary mainstays of many of the Atlantic tribes. Unlike the more typical New England clam chowder that uses dairy, this chowder, like many of the traditional ones of the Native peoples, has a clear broth that allows the briny, ocean taste of the hardshell clams called quahogs in the Northeast to come through more intensely. This chowder is seasoned simply with onion, dill, and some salt pork, a European addition to the pot and an indication of the early braiding of foodways, as it was often a staple on sailing ships. The chowder is made with a base of fish stock, and tastes of the salt air that surrounds Aquinnah.

6 ounces salt pork, rinsed and cut into ½-inch cubes

1 medium onion, finely chopped

½ teaspoon fennel seeds, crushed

2 cups chopped clams (I like to use Cento)

½ teaspoon brandy (optional)

1½ pounds russet potatoes, peeled and cut into ½-inch cubes

2 cups fish stock, store-bought or homemade (recipe follows)

1½ cups bottled clam juice

2 tablespoons minced fresh dill

Kosher salt and freshly ground black pepper

Crackers, for serving

1. In a Dutch oven, cook the salt pork over medium heat, stirring regularly, until browned and crisp, about 15 minutes. Using a slotted spoon, transfer the pork to a small bowl.

2. Remove all but 2 tablespoons of the rendered fat from the pot. Add the onions and fennel seeds, and cook, stirring occasionally, until the onions are softened, 10 to 15 minutes.

3. Increase the heat to high. Add the clams and brandy (if using) and cook, stirring constantly, for 2 minutes. Add the potatoes, fish stock, clam juice, 1 tablespoon of the dill, and reserved salt pork. Bring to a boil, then reduce the heat to maintain a simmer and cook until the potatoes are tender, about 15 minutes.

4. Taste and season with salt and pepper, if needed. Ladle into serving bowls, garnish with the remaining dill, and serve with crackers.

FISH STOCK

MAKES 1 QUART

Fish stock is a handy pantry item. Leftover stock can be used as a poaching liquid as well as in soups, stews, sauces, and risottos.

4 pounds fish bones (from white fish, such as flounder, bass, or halibut), cut into 2-inch pieces

1 cup dry white wine

2 cups chopped onions

5 medium celery stalks, coarsely chopped

4 medium carrots, coarsely chopped

Herb bundle: Bay leaves, parsley, and thyme sprigs (to taste), tied together with kitchen twine

Kosher salt

1. In a stockpot, combine the fish bones and water to cover by 1 to 2 inches. Add the wine and bring to a boil over high heat. Reduce the heat to low and skim off any white foam from the top. Add the vegetables and herb bundle and adjust the heat to let simmer. Cook for 25 minutes. Season lightly with salt, then strain the stock, discard the solids, and let it cool.

MUSTARD-AIOLI ROASTED BLUEFISH

SERVES 2

Bluefish is a popular game fish that is abundant in the waters off Martha's Vineyard. When the blues are running, they seem to be everywhere, but most often the fatty fish is found smoked. Juli cooks it fresh and attenuates the somewhat oily taste of the bluefish with a contemporary nod to European culinary traditions in the form of a lemony, mustardy aioli, spread on top before roasting, which also helps to keep the fish juicy. While the rich taste of bluefish is beloved by locals, this method also works well for other fish. Just make sure to adjust the cooking time if you have thinner fillets—they will cook faster.

2 skin-on bluefish fillets (6 ounces each)

Kosher salt and freshly ground black pepper

Vegetable oil or softened butter, for greasing

¼ cup mayonnaise

2 tablespoons fresh lemon juice

4 teaspoons Dijon mustard

½ teaspoon garlic powder

¼ teaspoon cayenne pepper

1. Preheat the oven to 400°F.

2. Pat the bluefish dry with paper towels and season with salt and black pepper on both sides. Grease a large skillet with the oil and place the fish skin-side down on it.

3. In a small bowl, whisk together the mayonnaise, lemon juice, mustard, garlic powder, and cayenne until combined. Coat the top of the fish fillets evenly with the mayonnaise mixture.

4. Roast until the bluefish flakes apart when gently prodded with a paring knife and registers 140°F, about 8 minutes. Serve hot.

WAMPANOAG CLAM FRITTERS

MAKES 8 LARGE OR 16 SMALL FRITTERS

Soft-shell clams, also called steamers because they are usually cooked that way, are somewhat difficult to obtain if you don't live in an area where the mollusks are abundant. They are worth the search in the same way that soft-shell crabs are; they are delicate in texture and briny in flavor. Be sure to pull off the tough outer coating of the siphon, which is a prominent feature of these clams.

Steamers are also known as Ipswich or Essex clams or, somewhat ironically, fryers, because that's the other way they are most often enjoyed.

If you cannot find steamers, substitute hard-shell littleneck clams, or even canned whole clams. The steamers are seasonal, showing up in the Northeast between May and October. Here, the clams' natural briny sweetness serves as a surprising foil for the tender fritter batter.

⅔ cup all-purpose flour

1 teaspoon baking powder

½ teaspoon kosher salt

½ teaspoon freshly ground black pepper

Minced fresh chives or cayenne pepper (optional)

⅓ cup whole milk

⅓ cup bottled clam juice or Fish Stock (page 27)

1 large egg

10 ounces freshly shucked clam meat, or 2 (10-ounce) cans baby clams (I like Cento brand), drained

2 cups vegetable oil, for frying

1. In a small bowl, whisk together the flour, baking powder, salt, and black pepper. If desired, stir in some chives or cayenne.

2. In a medium bowl, whisk together the milk, clam juice, and egg. Add the flour mixture and clam meats to the milk mixture and stir to combine.

3. In a medium Dutch oven or deep sauté pan, heat the oil over medium-high heat until it reaches 375°F. Adjust the heat as needed to maintain this temperature. Line a plate with paper towels and set near the stove.

4. Working in batches to avoid crowding, carefully spoon fritter batter into the hot oil and fry until golden brown on each side, 3 to 5 minutes, flipping halfway through cooking. Use ¼ cup batter for large fritters or 2 tablespoons for smaller ones. Transfer the fried fritters to the paper towels to drain. Serve hot.

THANKSGIVING

Entering the third decade of the twenty-first century, there is probably no American holiday more contentious than Thanksgiving. The holiday that became national by decree of President Abraham Lincoln in 1863, in the middle of the Civil War, is one that celebrates the much-fictionalized meeting between the Wampanoags and the Pilgrims. Today, we see with clearer eyes the problematic relations between the European settlers and the Indigenous people, leading to the eventual violent European conquest of the land. Of course, we also feel the momentum of ritual and celebration by millions of families who simply take the occasion toward the end of the fall to come together and feast.

But for a window on what could have been, it's worthwhile to read this passage by Edward Winslow who attended that first Thanksgiving in 1621:

> *Our harvest being gotten in, our governor sent four men on fowling, so that we might after a special manner rejoice together, after we had gathered the fruits of our labors; they four in one day killed as much fowl, as with a little help beside, served the Company almost a week, at which time amongst other recreations, we exercised our Arms, many of the Indians coming amongst us, and amongst the rest their greatest king Massasoit, with some ninety men, whom for three days we entertained and feasted, and they went out and killed five Deer, which they brought to the Plantation and bestowed on our governor, and upon the Captain and others. And although it be not always so plentiful, as it was at this time with us, yet by the goodness of God, we are so far from want, that we often wish you partakers of our plenty.*

We really don't know what they ate, although likely—as Juli Vanderhoop's recipes have shown—there were plentiful fish and clams, other shellfish, eels, and cranberries along with the corn, beans, and squash that the Wampanoag had taught the Pilgrims to grow using the Three Sisters method. The harmony evidenced by the gathering was short-lived, but it provides one of the very few examples of the potential of rapport between Europeans and Native peoples that we have from the early days of what would become the United States.

A NOTE ABOUT SALT

Salt is a complex matter in recipe writing. Savory dishes tend to be forgiving and while novice cooks should follow the recipe amounts, more adept cooks will often ignore them and salt to taste. Baking, however, is more complex and can go awry if the wrong salt is used. Morton's kosher salt is twice as salty as Diamond Crystal kosher salt. In the recipes in *Braided Heritage*, unless otherwise stated, Diamond Crystal kosher salt was used in development and testing.

RESERVATION REMEMBRANCES

RENÉE C. HUNTER

Renée C. Hunter breezed into my life as she sneaked out to my front porch on Martha's Vineyard to have a few puffs of a clandestine cigarette one summer's evening. I'd been entertaining an old friend that I had reconnected with on the island after forty years; Renée was her best friend and we found that we shared some history through her. I had been intrigued by her and was glad to have a few quiet minutes to speak with her. She was petite and elegant, wearing an armful of silver bracelets, jeans, and a top made stunning with a cashmere Hermès shawl, designed by Black Texan artist Kermit Oliver: an outfit that was multilayered, an interesting read. The Kermit Oliver shawl, I suspected, signaled that she might have some connection to the Native peoples that he illustrated so beautifully in his work. This suspicion was furthered by recognition of her wrought Navajo and Zuni bracelets, and eventually confirmed by Renée herself when she informed me that she was a fully enrolled member of the Shinnecock tribe.

As we got to know each other better, I learned that her father lived on the Shinnecock reservation on the eastern end of Long Island. I vaguely remembered the reservation as a small place, where I had gone to the annual Labor Day powwow when I was a small child. In those days, the reservation was nestled among the potato fields that were the agricultural mainstay of the region. Seventy years later, those potato fields have morphed into the enclave of the super-rich known as the Hamptons. Today, the small reservation is 1.3 square miles in the middle of that glossy enclave on Long Island's South Fork.

The Shinnecock, meaning People of the Shore, are closely related to the Pequot and the Mohegan and even share a common language. Like the Wampanoag of Martha's Vineyard, they live off the woodlands and the ocean and share many Atlantic coastal traditions and foodways with them.

Although she grew up mainly in Brooklyn and Queens, New York, Renée had spent summers out east, on the reservation, and in more recent times journeyed back there weekly to visit family, and to take care of her father. (Her father passed away while this book was being written, at over 104 years of age.)

Renée is a woman who blends past and present easily, while always remaining fiercely proud of her Native American origins. As one might easily surmise from her elegant presentation, she had a career in fashion, working first as a high fashion model in the

1960s, then in retail sales at Bloomingdale's and Saks Fifth Avenue, where she rose to become the fashion buyer for the Park Avenue Room and Advanced European Designers. After leaving Saks, she went into business for herself, and has taught courses in luxury goods at some of New York's fashion schools. Her links to the luxe world of style are apparent whenever she walks into a room.

As we spoke, though, it was less of the runways and the showrooms; she talked of her memories of the reservation in the autumn, the Labor Day powwow, one of the festivals that gave rhythm to her year. The word *powwow* comes from one of the nations of the Algonquian-speaking Northeast Indians. It describes a celebration of American Indian culture in which people from diverse nations gather for the purpose of dancing, singing, and honoring the traditions of their ancestors. For the Shinnecock powwow, tribes gather from as far away as the Dakotas, and traditional Shinnecock dishes are prepared that reflect the tribe's proximity to the water—with, as with the Wampanoag, the clam taking primacy of place.

Renée recalls many of the dishes that went with those traditional feasts. At the powwows, she remembers dishes from the ocean like a clear broth clam chowder, stuffed clams, clam pie, clam fritters. But in truth Renée is not the only cook in her family. Her sister, Roberta O. Hunter-Cuyjet, recalls the honor of being asked to bring her famed venison stew to the powwow. "We have a historic and cultural diet that includes venison; small game like raccoon, squirrel, and fox; wild birds like turkey, pheasant, and duck," she wrote to me, in addition to the fruits of the sea such as clams/quahogs, oysters, crabs, eel, and fish.

Venison has special meaning in her memories, as she described the colder months when the family would "dress down a deer," hanging the harvested animal from a tree:

> We carefully remove the whole hide to be dried, and eventually use it for clothes and traditional regalia. Throughout the years, the deer hunting season would mean early rising by my husband, brothers, cousin, and friends to position themselves in the right spots to greet the ghostlike figures in the forests. Traditionally, it is important to give thanks when taking the life of our four-legged relatives. It is always with reverence that sage and/or sweetgrass is burned while the deer is being dressed down. It is an honor to be gifted a portion of venison meat.

In winter, Renée especially remembers samp, which was dried whole hominy corn, cooked perhaps with a piece of "streak of lean"—fat pork—and possibly some onions. It might be seasoned with a bay leaf and some black pepper, but the seasonings were basic, focusing on the rich flavor of nixtamalized corn—the same beguiling flavor you find in fresh corn tortillas. Although it was also served at the autumn powwow, samp was most definitely a dish served through the winter, using corn that was dried for preservation, and it was served often with biscuits or freshly baked bread. Again, the use of wheat flour signals the early contact with Europeans and the early and deep roots of the American braid. Dried beans were also important in the diet—navy, kidney, and black-eyed peas.

In springtime, the community looked forward to the June Meeting, held the first Sunday in June to celebrate planting time and the first tastes of warmer weather. The culinary star of that time would always be strawberries, which Renée remembers were featured in fresh strawberry shortcakes.

But as she spent summers on the reservation, the heat of the hot months is what brings her back home. Summer was also about clams, as well as mussels, sweet corn, tomatoes, cucumbers, and potatoes. "We had potatoes because Long Island used to be the potato capital of America until Idaho hired a PR person. Potatoes are a Native American food—just Native South American," she remarks, laughing.

We had them baked, roasted, fried, just about any way you can serve them. It was also big blueberry country out there and so there was something called blueberry slump. It was a very soft dumpling that was covered with cooked blueberries.

While both men and women cooked, as in many parts of the traditional world, some Shinnecock foods were gendered. Men tended to work with open flame, while women tended stews and baked. In summer, there were also clambakes:

Clambakes were men's work 'cause they would go out and dig the hole. Then the hole got lined with stones. They'd put the potatoes in first and then layer it all up in order: potatoes, corn, clams, and the rest. The men did that kind of stuff. Women baked. There were other dishes like venison chili that might be a crossover thing that could be made by men or women.

Clams are like medicine to me, it's like some kind of spiritual thing. Even in New York City I'll go across the street to the fish market, buy a dozen clams, and come home.

Clams, potatoes, corn, those things mean the reservation for me.

THE THREE SISTERS

In many Native traditional communities, corn was often grown in symbiotic harmony with squash and beans. The corn stalks provide a place for the bean plants to climb. The bean vines root the corn plants to the ground and keep the stalks from falling over, blowing down, or washing away. The beans also fix nitrogen in the soil, to fertilize the plants. These young plants are shaded by the squash leaves, which allow the soil to retain moisture; the prickly stems of squash plants serve to keep critters from nibbling the corn and beans. Grown in agricultural harmony, the three plants became the mainstay for many of the Iroquoian groups, and is hence known as the Iroquoian Triad . . . or more popularly the Three Sisters. While all elements of the triad turned up on the table in various forms, they were often combined in a succotash: a dish that takes its name from the Narragansett *sukquttahash* or *msickquatash,* a term meaning "broken or boiled corn kernels."

The oldest of the Three Sisters is squash, a Native American plant that probably originated in Central America or Mexico around 7000 to 5000 BCE. It was domesticated some eight thousand years ago, before corn, and migrated north; it had reached as far north as the land that would become Canada before European contact. The vegetable got its English name from the Narragansett word *askatasquash,* which means "eaten raw or uncooked"—though the squashes were often eaten in soups and stews, or roasted in animal fats. Immature plants, as well as leaves, flowers, and seeds were also eaten.

Because they cross-pollinate quite easily, there are seemingly endless varieties of squash. Everything from the gourds that make maracas to the pumpkin that is carved on Halloween are members of the squash family.

Squash was one of the foods introduced to the European colonists by the Native peoples and was adopted early by them. The earliest known American recipe in English for it is one for pumpkin pudding—in *American Cookery* (1796) by Amelia Simmons—an early version of today's pumpkin pie.

The third part of the Iroquoian triad and the third of the Three Sisters is the bean. The distinctions between beans and peas are so thorny that attempting to untangle them is best left to botanists. Many beans are native to the Americas and were domesticated separately in ancient Mesoamerica and also in the Andes. They include such species as pinto beans, kidney beans, black beans, lima beans, and even our green beans. They complete the triad, and when prepared together with the corn and squash with which they were traditionally planted, they provide an exceptionally balanced meal comprising proteins, carbohydrates, healthy fats, and vitamins. That is the magic of the Three Sisters.

CLAM PIE

SERVES 4

This unusual pie is like a chicken pot pie, but uses the clams that are abundant on the East Coast. It's a simple filling of just a few ingredients, but the savoriness of chicken is replaced with the brininess of clams; salt pork or bacon adds richness, and potatoes bring heft. This is rustic fare, but the presentation can be special when you cut into the crust, releasing the steam and aroma. Again, the use of wheat flour for the crust indicates an adaptation of European foodways, and is another example of the prevalence of the American braid.

4 ounces salt pork or bacon, cut into small bite-sized pieces

1 medium onion, cut into small bite-sized pieces

1½ pounds Yukon Gold potatoes, peeled and cut into small bite-sized pieces

Kosher salt and freshly ground black pepper

2 dozen freshly shucked clams, cut into small bite-sized pieces, or 2 (10-ounce) cans baby clams (I like Cento), drained

1 (8-ounce) bottle clam juice

Store-bought refrigerated pie dough for one 9-inch deep-dish pie

1. In a large sauté pan or Dutch oven, sauté the salt pork over medium heat until rendered and soft, about 5 minutes. Do not brown.

2. Pour off some of the fat if desired, but leave enough to cook the onions and potatoes. Add the onions to the pan and cook, stirring until softened and translucent, but do not brown, 3 to 5 minutes.

3. Preheat the oven to 375°F.

4. Add the potatoes to the salt pork/onion mixture and continue to cook, stirring regularly, until the potatoes are tender but not fully soft, 12 to 15 minutes. Season with salt and pepper. Stir in the clams, clam juice, and salt and pepper to taste.

5. Place the filling in a 1 to 1½-inch deep 9-inch pie pan or a casserole dish and cover with the pie dough. Crimp or fold over the edges.

6. Bake until the crust is cooked through and well browned, about 30 minutes. Let cool slightly and serve warm.

SAMP

SERVES 8

Samp is a winter dish: a satisfying stew of dried hominy that is mainly served from October to March. It is a toothsome no-frills dish that is stick-to-the-ribs hearty. It's simple, but with good ingredients, the flavor shines. Prepared from whole kernels of dried field corn that have been nixtamalized (a process by which the kernels are soaked in a lye solution, then rinsed to unlock their nutrients), it tastes like the aroma of good corn tortillas, and Renée craves it in the winter as her warming and memory-filled comfort food. Sioux chef Sean Sherman (see page 62) explains that hominy is "the building block of Indigenous foods in many parts of North America—it's the basis for tortillas, tamales, and all the masa products that are the staff of life in Mexico and beyond."

According to settler Roger Williams, the word "samp" is an anglicization of the Narragansett word *nasàump*. This is one of the recipes that results from the corn, beans, and squash growing patterns—the combination of corn and beans forms a complete protein, and the Three Sisters grow together in the field while protecting one another. It's so traditional to Long Island that in 1986, *New York Times* dining critic Craig Claiborne and chef Pierre Franey published a recipe for Long Island Country Samp from chef Larry Forgione. Some folks add milk to the stew as it is served. Others doctor it up with hot sauce. Either way, it becomes a full meal when served with biscuits or corn bread.

Because of the simplicity of this recipe, quality ingredients are key; try to find the beans and hominy from a specialty purveyor, such as Rancho Gordo.

1 pound dried navy beans

1 pound dried whole hominy

4 to 8 ounces any smoked meat (such as ham, ham bone, or smoked turkey legs)

1 large onion, diced

2 or 3 bay leaves

Kosher salt

1. In a large pot, combine the beans and hominy with enough water to cover by 1 to 2 inches and soak them overnight.

2. The next day, drain off the soaking water and add fresh water to come 3 inches above the beans and hominy. Add the smoked meat, onion, and bay leaves. Bring to a boil over high heat. Reduce to a simmer, partially cover, and cook until the beans and hominy are tender, about 2 hours. Check the pot occasionally and add water if the water level goes below the surface of the beans. You want enough water for a stew-like consistency in the end.

3. During the last few minutes of cooking, season to taste with salt. Remove any bones (if used). You can also pull out the smoked meat and chop it up, returning it to the pot, if you'd like. Serve hot.

VENISON STEW

SERVES 4 TO 6

Deer abounded and venison was a major source of animal protein for many Native peoples. Here, the venison is prepared in a hearty stew of red wine, tomatoes, abundant seasonings, and, if you're inclined, cream. Cooked until tender, the lean venison is well flavored and wonderful with rice. This recipe came from Renée's sister, Roberta O. Hunter-Cuyjet, who is often asked to bring this stew to many of the Shinnecock gatherings, including the annual powwow, the harvest gathering of Nunnowa, and the midwinter celebration held around the full moon of late January or February.

MARINATED VENISON

1 cup dry red wine

1 tablespoon kosher salt

3 tablespoons olive oil

1 tablespoon balsamic vinegar

2 teaspoons Worcestershire sauce

1 teaspoon dried sage

1 bay leaf

2½ pounds venison meat, cut into 1½-inch cubes

1 tablespoon pickling spices

STEW

2 cups all-purpose flour, or as needed

Olive oil, as needed

2 medium onions, diced

3 medium celery stalks, diced

2 garlic cloves, minced

2½ cups beef or vegetable broth

½ teaspoon freshly ground black pepper, plus more to taste

1 teaspoon garlic powder

1 bay leaf

1 teaspoon dried basil

1 teaspoon dried oregano

1½ pounds carrots (about 4 large), scrubbed well and diced

Kosher salt

1 (14.5-ounce) can stewed tomatoes

1½ pounds Yukon Gold potatoes (about 4 medium), peeled and medium-diced

4 ounces sliced mushrooms

1 cup red wine

1 cup heavy cream (optional)

Cooked rice, for serving

(recipe continues)

1. **MARINATE THE VENISON:** In a large baking dish or ziplock bag, combine the red wine, salt, olive oil, balsamic vinegar, Worcestershire sauce, sage, bay leaf, and venison.

2. Securely wrap the pickling spices in cheesecloth and tie it tight with kitchen twine. Place the spice pouch in the marinade and make sure it's submerged in liquid.

3. Place the venison in the refrigerator to marinate for at least 8 and up to 24 hours.

4. **MAKE THE STEW:** Remove the venison from the marinade, discarding the marinade and the pickling spice pouch. Pat the venison dry with paper towels.

5. Place the venison in a large bowl and toss with the flour to coat (you may not need all the flour).

6. In a large Dutch oven, heat a healthy splash of olive oil over medium heat until it shimmers. Working in batches to not crowd the pot, add enough venison to just cover the bottom and cook, turning, until browned all over, 3 to 4 minutes per side. Place the venison on a large plate and repeat until all the meat is well browned.

7. Add the onions and celery and an additional splash of oil if needed to the pot, stirring so that the vegetables pick up the browned bits stuck on the bottom. Cook, stirring occasionally, until soft and almost translucent, 5 to 7 minutes. Add the garlic and cook for an additional 30 seconds, until fragrant.

8. Stir in the broth, pepper, garlic powder, bay leaf, basil, oregano, carrots, and venison. Cover and bring to a simmer. Reduce the heat to low and cook, covered, until the venison is tender, about 2½ hours.

9. Taste the stew and add salt and pepper as needed. Add the stewed tomatoes and potatoes and increase the heat to a simmer. Reduce it back to low and cook until the sauce thickens slightly, about 30 minutes more.

10. Add the sliced mushrooms, red wine, and cream (if using) and cook for an additional 30 minutes, or until the venison is fork-tender. Taste and add more salt and pepper as needed. Serve with rice.

POWWOWS

Tribal gatherings have long been traditional in North American Native cultures. However, the English term "powwow" comes from a mispronunciation of the Narrick word *Pau Wau* from the Algonquian peoples, designating a shaman or healer, and by extension came to mean a gathering of them in ceremony.

Modern powwows have their origin in tribal gatherings that resulted from attempts to counteract the destruction, forced migration, and uprooting of many of the Plains Indian tribes and were originally a way of banding together to maintain cultural traditions. By the beginning of the twentieth century, with the advent of nontribal Wild West shows and their usurpation and appropriation for profit of tribal cultures, the term was devalued.

Now, however, the word "powwow" has been reclaimed by First Peoples and has come to mean a gathering of different tribes that can take place from one to four days. These powwows are held around the country, and often draw participants from hundreds of miles away who may be dancers, singers, artists, artisans, or traders. The dances that are performed at powwows are derived from gatherings that go back to before European contact and are usually associated with religious ceremonies, celebrations commemorating successful battles, celebrations of political and or territorial alliances, and events that are sponsored by family groups. While traditional celebrations gathered people from neighboring regions, contemporary powwows are much more inclusive and may involve members of multiple tribes with visitors coming long distances and even from other countries: a gathering of solidarity celebrating Indigenousness. The largest powwow in North America is the Gathering of Nations in Albuquerque, New Mexico, which is held at the end of April. It brings together more than five hundred tribes from America and more than two hundred tribes from Canada.

STRAWBERRY SHORTCAKE

SERVES 4

The June Meeting with the Shinnecock Presbyterian Church—one of the oldest Presbyterian Missions in the United States, is a gathering that celebrates springtime, planting time, and remembrance of the departed. It is song and worship on the first Sunday in June. This feast day is also the time of the first ripened wild strawberries and blueberries, and Shinnecock strawberry shortcake takes center stage in each home to welcome family and friends. This recipe features simple buttermilk drop biscuits, served with a sweet strawberry compote—left uncooked to preserve the berries' fresh flavor—and whipped cream. The simplicity of this recipe means that the quality of the ingredients is paramount; use the sweetest, juiciest in-season strawberries you can find.

Vegetable oil, for greasing

1½ cups plus 1 tablespoon all-purpose flour

2 tablespoons granulated sugar

1½ teaspoons baking powder

⅛ teaspoon baking soda

½ teaspoon kosher salt

¼ cup buttermilk, at room temperature

¾ cup heavy cream, at room temperature

TO FINISH

1 cup heavy cream

Powdered sugar (optional)

Strawberry Compote (recipe follows)

1. Preheat the oven to 400°F. Line a baking sheet with parchment paper and lightly grease the paper with the oil.

2. In a medium bowl, stir together the flour, 1 tablespoon of the granulated sugar, the baking powder, baking soda, and salt.

3. In a liquid measuring cup, combine the buttermilk and heavy cream. Add to the flour mixture, stirring and folding just until a batter forms. Grease a ⅓-cup dry measure and scoop 8 biscuits onto the prepared pan. Sprinkle them with the remaining 1 tablespoon granulated sugar.

4. Bake until the tops are golden brown, about 15 minutes.

5. **TO FINISH:** In a bowl, with an electric mixer, beat the cold heavy cream until soft peaks form. If desired, sweeten to taste with powdered sugar.

6. Serve the shortcakes warm, split open and topped with the strawberry compote to taste and whipped cream.

STRAWBERRY COMPOTE

MAKES ABOUT 1½ CUPS

This very simple-to-prepare strawberry compote is not only an essential component of the strawberry shortcake, it can also be prepared separately and used as a topping for ice cream.

1 pint strawberries, hulled and quartered

½ cup granulated sugar

1 tablespoon fresh lemon juice

1. In a medium bowl, combine the strawberries, granulated sugar, lemon juice, and 2 teaspoons water. Toss gently until the sugar has dissolved. Allow the berries to macerate for 30 minutes, stirring every 10 minutes, until they are tender and their juice has formed a natural syrup.

CULTURE WARRIOR

JOHN BARBRY

John Barbry is the director of development and planning for the Tunica-Biloxi tribe of Louisiana, and as such, he oversees their culture and language revitalization program. For this reason, he has chosen to add the names of the recipes he's shared not only in French-inflected English, but in the Tunica language as well. Today's Tunica-Biloxi tribal nation comprises Tunica, Biloxi, Ofo, Avoyel, and Choctaw people. The last fluent Tunica speaker died more than half a century ago, but thanks to the efforts of John Barbry—and people like him working in conjunction with a team of anthropologists and linguists from Tulane University—there are now sixty people speaking Tunica with varying degrees of fluency.

A self-defined "cultural warrior," Barbry works to showcase Tunica culture through demonstrations at places like the annual New Orleans Jazz and Heritage Festival (Jazz Fest) and The Historic New Orleans Collection. He grew up on the reservation near Marksville, Louisiana, and describes the state of that culture as he saw it:

Like a lot of Native American communities, our heritage, our culture, our language, and our oral traditions were interrupted by colonial contact. When my father was growing up, he spoke French; everybody spoke French here. The Tunica and the Biloxi languages were only known by some of the elders. And that was fading when my father grew up in the forties and fifties. The last fluent speaker of the Tunica language died in 1948, right after my father was born. So we were very assimilated. We were an Indian community with several different cultures. The Tunica were the southernmost Indian Nation. They migrated down the Mississippi trying to get away from the British—and the other tribes who were slave-hunting for them. We met up with other groups and banded together for protection. . . . Eventually we became one Native American community. We encountered the French in 1699, and developed a relationship based on a mutual enmity for the British-armed and -inspired Chickasaw slave traders. This alliance engendered a move further down from the

Yazoo Basin midway to New Orleans so we've had that relationship for a long time. I'm sure there are things that contribute to the cuisine that come from both cultures, but it's kind of hard to break them apart.

The Tunica became the middlemen in a salt trade to the French. As many Native traditions had come together in the creation of the tribe, so many culinary traditions had also merged to form the recipes that Barbry and his community celebrate today as their own. As with tribes of first contact in the Northeast, the mixing or colonizing of culinary traditions came early. The French also intermarried with Native peoples (which was more unusual in the areas that were controlled by the British), resulting in even more combining of foodways. The mixing still continues in Barbry's family; Barbry's father, who was "from the tribal side," and his paternal grandmother as well as his great-aunts, who were French, could all cook a sauce "gravy" as it is called in the area: rich stews and fricassées of chicken or pork thickened with roux. There is a local adage to describe the beginnings of cooking any meal: "First put on a pot of rice." Rice, a staple crop of Louisiana, was the great provider; it could always stretch even a modest amount of "gravy" to feed the family or unexpected guests. It was always on the stove in a cast-iron pot. If other family members dropped in, his grandmother would bake another pan of biscuits and somehow it would stretch to serve all.

Much of the food that Barbry speaks of would be thought of by many as simply variations of traditional country food of southern Louisiana known as Cajun, and indeed often the distinctions are so subtle as to be unrecognizable to all but the cognoscenti. They often depend on less-expensive cuts of meat as with the meatballs or the chicken gizzard jambalaya, but they signal changes in income, lifestyle, and history. While many think of the food of southern Louisiana in general as spicy hot, seasoning for John was simple and largely depended on salt, red pepper, garlic powder, shallots, and scallions, as well as the combination of celery, green bell pepper, and onion known in the hugely Roman Catholic region as the Holy Trinity. Vegetables usually came from family gardens and ranged from cucumbers and tomatoes to sweet potatoes, especially the beloved white sweet potatoes, which had a creamier flavor and are not as sweet as the red-skinned ones. There was also corn, from which they made a dish called maque choux, a mix of corn, bell peppers, and onion. And field peas, and okra, often sautéed. All this was served with, of course, rice, but also corn bread or with what they call galettes, a simple biscuit fried in a cast-iron skillet rather than baked.

Pork was a dietary staple. Barbry likes to joke that while Hernando de Soto encountered the Tunica early on and brought devastating disease, he can at least be credited for introducing pork to the diet. And so, in May, the annual Cochon de Lait festival, a feast of suckling pig, in Mansura, Louisiana, remains a high point of the year for the community.

Pigs that grew to maturity were also eaten; they were butchered in the winter. At home, Barbry remembers hog-killing time being around Christmastime in his family, when the temperatures are relatively cooler and the danger of spoilage is somewhat reduced. At that point, hog's head cheese, both red and white boudin—a meaty rice mixture stuffed in a casing (the red one contains pig's blood)—would be prepared. The meat would be dressed, prepared for winter, and distributed to family and friends. Cracklin's, slowly-crisped pig skin (known in Cajun dialect as gratons) are also made. All of these treats, once annual, are now available at roadside stands throughout southern Louisiana all year-round and some are celebrated in routes designed for culinary tourism, like the Southern Boudin Trail created by the Southern Foodways Alliance.

As Barbry describes the food of his childhood and the food of his family's culinary traditions, he recalls that these were not fancy meals, but rather subsistence cooking made tasty and delicious through the ingenuity of his relatives. Speaking of one of his aunts, he says, "She used to brag about how her favorite part of the chicken was the neck bone. If you know, there's not a whole lot of meat on neck bones, but that was just her being of good humor and generous of spirit. We just took it all in stride. We were feeding everybody."

The recipes that exist today were all a part of the oral tradition of the individual families, and by extension the tribe. But, as with much of oral tradition, it is fragile and one of the things that Barbry works on is recalling and remembering and reconstructing traditions from collective tribal memory. He speaks of his own family:

> I've known grandmas and others who keep little index cards and write things down, but in my family, I don't think it was necessarily "cooking as an art." You know, we down in Louisiana say, "Instead of eating to live, we live to eat." But back in my grandma's day, when I was a kid, it was something that was done not really out of fun. I don't think any of it was written down. So when I talk about recipes, those are really just handed down orally.

Oral traditions, of course, can attenuate, or even die out when not consciously maintained. That is something that many of the non-European foundational cultures of the United States must deal with, in claiming their part of the American braid and in maintaining their culinary and cultural heritage—to ensure that these traditions are being rekindled, revitalized, and decolonialized. And to ensure that new generations are learning from their old cultures and rebuilding their cultural heritages anew, we need cultural warriors like John Barbry, whose recipes hark back to the tribal foods he remembers from his grandmother's table, after centuries of tribal ingenuity braided with that of the French.

BEEF BOULETTES AND GRAVY
YANISHITISHUMA TOLU TISHK''ƐMA

SERVES 4 TO 6

For John Barbry, beef was expensive while growing up, and so was eaten infrequently. When it was, it was sometimes in the form of beef meatballs that are called boulettes, served with a gravy-like broth. It is interesting to note that many of the Tunica-Biloxi dishes that John Barbry offers have similar cooking methods and taste profiles. It's important to remember that these dishes often originated as make-do dishes that were created in adversity to get taste and nourishment from inexpensive ingredients, and through ingenuity, certain methods were developed or embraced that created delicious sustenance.

Many of the dishes are also served with white rice. In the Tunica language, rice was called *onrↃwahushoku,* which means "white man's corn," an interesting look at how etymology often tells history. Corn, a Native American grain, was undoubtedly the preeminent traditional grain. However, as rice production in Louisiana grew in the mid-nineteenth century, with the area taking primacy in milling and marketing from South Carolina, rice took over on local tables as well. Rice was brought to this land by Europeans, but worked by enslaved Africans and their descendants, who brought expertise in rice cultivation, as the grain had been a staple in some West African diets for over three millennia.

BOULETTES

- 3 pounds lean ground beef
- 1 teaspoon kosher salt, plus more as needed
- 1 teaspoon finely ground black pepper
- 1 teaspoon sugar
- 1 teaspoon garlic powder
- 1 tablespoon dried onion
- 1 tablespoon chopped fresh parsley
- ½ cup bread crumbs
- ¼ teaspoon cayenne pepper

GRAVY

- 5 tablespoons vegetable oil
- 2 large yellow onions, chopped
- 3 large garlic cloves, chopped
- 1 small green bell pepper, chopped
- 1 teaspoon kosher salt, plus more to taste
- 1 teaspoon finely ground black pepper
- 1 teaspoon sugar
- 1 teaspoon garlic powder
- ¼ teaspoon cayenne pepper
- 4 heaping tablespoons Roux (page 57), cooled

FOR SERVING

- ¼ cup chopped fresh parsley
- 1 small bunch of scallions, chopped
- Cooked rice, for serving

(recipe continues)

1. Preheat the oven to 350°F. Grease a sheet pan or 9 × 13-inch baking pan with cooking spray.

2. **MAKE THE BOULETTES:** In a large bowl, combine the ground beef, salt, black pepper, sugar, garlic powder, dried onion, parsley, bread crumbs, and cayenne.

3. Take a heaping tablespoon of the meat mixture to form each boulette (meatball) with your hands (wetting if needed). Arrange the boulettes on the pan.

4. Bake until browned and firm, about 45 minutes.

5. Remove from the oven; tilt the pan over a heatproof bowl just enough to drain off any rendered fat. Allow the boulettes to cool.

6. **MAKE THE GRAVY:** In an 8-quart Dutch oven, heat the oil over medium heat until shimmering but not smoking, about 4 minutes.

7. Stir in the onions, garlic, and bell pepper and cook, stirring occasionally, until the vegetables are softened and lightly browned, 15 to 20 minutes.

8. Add the cooled boulettes to the pot. Season with the salt, black pepper, sugar, garlic powder, and cayenne. Add 2½ quarts water, increase the heat to high, cover, and cook for 20 minutes, gently stirring the boulettes every 5 minutes (keeping them whole and covered in between stirrings).

9. Reduce the heat to medium-high and stir in the roux, making sure it is well incorporated. Cover and cook for 30 minutes or until the sauce slightly thickens. The meatballs should be completely coated in the sauce.

10. Reduce the heat to medium, stir gently, and partially cover, and cook for 30 minutes.

11. Uncover, and cook until the level of liquid is slightly less than the top of the boulettes, about 20 minutes. By this time, the liquid should have thickened into a gravy, and the boulettes should be very tender. Taste and add salt as desired.

12. **TO SERVE:** Gently stir in the chopped parsley and scallions and serve with rice.

PAN-FRIED GALETTES
HAHKAMUCHI MAKASAMANI

SERVES 6

Pan-fried galettes are something John Barbry enjoyed growing up, often cooked by his father. The word *galette* comes from the French, indicating a flat round pastry or cake, but its Tunica name, *hahkamuchi madasamani*, is a bit more precise, literally "bread, grease-cooked." It's a simple biscuit dough, formed into a small pancake and fried in a little bit of oil, in a cast-iron skillet. His father would cook them for breakfast mainly, and of course he'd put syrup or jam on them. They are also wonderful served as a bread alongside vegetables, such as field peas.

2 cups self-rising flour, plus more for dusting

Kosher salt

¼ cup vegetable shortening

¾ cup whole milk

Vegetable oil, for frying

1. Place the flour and a few generous pinches of salt into a bowl. With a pastry cutter or two knives, or using your fingertips, cut in the vegetable shortening until little lumps of shortening are mixed within the flour. Slowly stir in the milk until a dough forms and comes free from the sides of the bowl.

2. Lightly flour a clean work surface and dump the dough onto it. Gently knead 3 or 4 times, until smooth. Reflour the surface and roll the dough out to a ¼-inch thickness. Cut the dough into 3-inch rounds with a flour-dusted biscuit cutter or a floured drinking glass. Gather the dough scraps, reroll, and cut out more dough rounds.

3. Warm an 8- or 10-inch skillet (seasoned cast iron or nonstick work well) over medium-high heat. Add enough oil to generously coat the pan and heat until the oil is shimmering-hot.

4. Place as many rounds of dough as will fit comfortably in one layer in the pan and cook until golden brown, about 2 minutes. Use a spatula and flip to brown the other side, about 2 minutes. The galettes will fluff as they cook. Remove the galettes and place on a plate or serving platter. You may place the platter in a warm oven to keep warm while cooking the rest.

5. Re-oil the pan and repeat cooking until all the dough is used. They are best served warm.

CHICKEN GIZZARD JAMBALAYA
CHƆHPALAYA KAPASHI UNISHARA

SERVES 6 TO 8

Jambalaya, the southern Louisiana classic, is known to many from Hank Williams's famous song "Jambalaya (On the Bayou)." John Barbry's jambalaya—despite sharing the western name—is not the well-known chicken and red rice dish. That jambalaya is thought to have West African antecedents in the thieboudienne of Senegal and the jollof rices of Ghana and Nigeria, where the red color of the rice originally came from the use of rich palm nut oil, but today often comes from tomatoes.

This version, though, is a delicious, meaty rendition that is essentially a rich, tomatoless, roux-based gravy loaded with smoked sausage and chicken gizzards, folded into rice. Labeled as an "off cut" and inexpensive, gizzards are very chewy when quickly cooked. However, when slowly cooked until tender, they have a very deep, rich "dark-meat" chicken flavor, and are high in protein and low in fat.

1 pound chicken gizzards

1 teaspoon kosher salt, plus more to taste

1 teaspoon freshly ground black pepper

¼ teaspoon cayenne pepper

1 teaspoon garlic powder

2 tablespoons Louisiana-style hot sauce

¼ cup vegetable oil

2 large yellow onions, chopped

4 large garlic cloves, chopped

1 small green bell pepper, chopped

½ cup chopped celery

1 pound smoked pork sausage (or beef or mixed sausage), cut into thin half-moons

4 heaping tablespoons Roux (recipe follows), cooled

1 small bunch of scallions, chopped

1 tablespoon chopped fresh parsley

4 to 5 cups cooked white rice, for serving

1. Rinse the chicken gizzards and remove any thin red or yellow membranes from their edges.

2. In an 8-quart Dutch oven, combine the gizzards, 3 cups water, the salt, black pepper, cayenne, garlic powder, and hot sauce. Cover and cook over medium heat until soft, 4 to 5 hours, stirring every 20 minutes. (Alternatively, you can cook them in a slow cooker on high for 7 hours.)

3. Uncover, transfer to a large bowl, and let cool.

4. In an 8-quart cast-iron pot or Dutch oven, heat the oil over medium heat until shimmering but not smoking. Stir in the onions, garlic, bell pepper, and celery and cook, stirring occasionally, until the vegetables are softened and lightly browned, 15 to 20 minutes.

5. Add the gizzards and their broth. Increase the heat to medium-high, stir in the smoked sausage, and simmer for 15 minutes.

6. Stir in the roux, making sure it's well incorporated. Cover and cook for 15 minutes more.

7. Reduce the heat to medium, stir in the scallions and parsley, and cook until the liquid level is slightly less than the level of meat in the pot, 10 to 15 minutes.

8. Gently stir in the cooked rice (to taste), until completely incorporated. Season to taste with salt. Remove from the heat and let sit covered for 15 minutes. Uncover and stir once more to evenly distribute the meat and vegetables. Serve.

ROUX
MAKES 2 CUPS

The roux may be used hot in cold liquids, or cooled or cold in hot liquids. You will need roux to make the Beef Boulettes and Gravy (page 51) and Pork Stew (page 59).

1 cup vegetable oil   1 cup all-purpose flour

1. In a small cast-iron skillet, heat the oil over medium heat until shimmering but not smoking. Using a large metal spoon, gradually stir in the flour a little at a time, and cook, stirring constantly, until the mixture is medium to dark brown, 4 to 5 minutes; do not leave unattended. When dark brown, transfer the roux to a heatproof bowl. Use right away, or cover and store in the refrigerator for 2 to 3 weeks.

PORK STEW
IYUT'ɛ TISHKI

SERVES 6 TO 8

The term *fricassée* in French describes a stew comprising pieces of meat that are seared or pan-fried and then braised in stock and served in a white sauce. It's a classic country dish that goes back to the fourteenth century in France. Over the years, it became French comfort food, and as such migrated to the United States with French explorers and settlers where it could be prepared from easily obtained ingredients, like pork.

3 pounds trimmed boneless Boston butt (pork shoulder)

2 teaspoons kosher salt, plus more to taste

1 teaspoon finely ground black pepper

1 teaspoon garlic powder

¼ teaspoon cayenne pepper

5 tablespoons vegetable oil

2 large yellow onions, chopped

4 large garlic cloves, chopped

1 small green bell pepper, chopped

½ cup chopped celery

4 heaping tablespoons Roux (page 57), cooled

Chopped scallions, for serving

Cooked rice, for serving

1. Cut the pork into 1½-inch pieces. Season with the salt, black pepper, garlic powder, and cayenne.

2. In an 8-quart Dutch oven, heat the oil over medium heat until shimmering but not smoking. Add the pork and increase the heat to medium-high. Cook, stirring thoroughly every 5 minutes, until evenly browned, about 30 minutes total. Transfer to a plate.

3. To the pot, add the onions, garlic, bell pepper, and celery and cook, stirring occasionally, until the vegetables have caramelized, 15 to 20 minutes.

4. Return the pork and any accumulated juices to the pot. Stir in 2½ quarts water, cover, and bring to a simmer. Stir in the roux, making sure it is well incorporated. Cover and cook for 15 minutes more.

5. Uncover and stir thoroughly. Reduce the heat to medium, partially cover, and cook until the liquid has thickened into a gravy and the pork is fork-tender, about 1 hour 20 minutes. (If the liquid level cooks down below the meat level, add enough water to just cover the meat.)

6. Taste and add more salt as necessary, add the scallions, and serve with rice.

CHICKEN FRICASSÉE
KAPASHI TISHKI

SERVES 4

This chicken stew is very similar to the Pork Stew (page 59) but uses chicken, which was a bit more common. Chicken fricassée has become a classic comfort food in Cajun country. Interestingly, a variant of this recipe turns up on Leni Sorensen's African American table in Southern California (see page 155), in testimonial to the early blending of foodways and ingredients.

1 whole chicken (3 to 3½ pounds)

1 teaspoon kosher salt

1 teaspoon finely ground black pepper

1 teaspoon garlic powder

¼ teaspoon cayenne pepper

5 tablespoons vegetable oil

1 tablespoon sugar

2 large yellow onions, chopped

3 large garlic cloves, chopped

1 small green bell pepper, chopped

1 tablespoon chopped fresh parsley

1 small bunch of scallions, chopped

Cooked rice, for serving

1. Cut the chicken into 10 pieces: drumsticks, wings, thighs, each breast split in half. (Include the gizzard, liver, heart, and neck, if available.) Do not remove any skin. Season with the salt, black pepper, garlic powder, and cayenne.

2. In an 8-quart Dutch oven, heat the oil over medium heat until shimmering but not smoking. Add the chicken pieces, increase the heat to high, and cook for 10 minutes, flipping the pieces once or twice, to get a rich brown.

3. Sprinkle the sugar evenly over the chicken pieces and cook over medium-low heat, gently stirring every 4 or 5 minutes, until the chicken is the color of light caramel, 20 to 25 minutes. Transfer all the pieces to a plate.

4. To the pot, add the onions, garlic, and bell pepper. Increase the heat to medium-high and cook, stirring occasionally, until the vegetables are soft and lightly browned, 15 to 20 minutes.

5. Return all the browned chicken pieces to the pot, add 1½ quarts water (or chicken stock), cover, and cook for 15 minutes.

6. Uncover and stir gently. Reduce the heat to medium, partially cover, and cook until the liquid has thickened into a light gravy and the meat is fork-tender and starting to separate from the bones, about 40 minutes. (If the level of liquid has cooked down to below the level of chicken, add water to top up.)

7. Add the parsley and scallions and serve hot with rice.

THE SIOUX CHEF

SEAN SHERMAN

Judging by the fanfare surrounding the opening of several new Indigenous restaurants around the country, the food of Native Americans is beginning to gain well-deserved (albeit way-too-late) acknowledgment in the world of food in the United States. That is in no small part due to the pioneering work of Native American food activist Sean Sherman, whose company is named, cleverly, The Sioux Chef.

The humorous irony of his nom de cuisine belies Sean's seriousness of mission. His restaurant Owamni, which was crowned with the James Beard Award for Best New Restaurant in 2022, was designed to celebrate Indigenous history, and reimagine its present. It is conceptualized as a "decolonized" restaurant and is on Owámniyomni, land sacred to the Dakota and Anishinaabe people, situated near present-day downtown Minneapolis. Decolonizing the food of his people means the creation of a cuisine that could have been—his food draws on old and contemporary Indigenous foodways, created without any of the ingredients brought here by colonization. In a sense, he is seeking to "unbraid" Indigenous food from the European and African threads, and is creating both very old dishes, and very new ones that rely on Indigenous ingredients inflected by today's

kitchen techniques and know-how. Topping countless "best restaurant" lists, Owamni presents a feast without wheat, refined sugar, pork, beef, chicken, and myriad other common ingredients, relying entirely on a pantry that would have been available to Indigenous people—and showcasing that delicious bounty.

This work involves not only the talents of a chef, but adds to those skills historical and anthropological research, botanical investigation, and works of deep memory recalling what he and others have learned and heard from elders long gone. His mission continues to inspire others, and in 2023, he was named one of *TIME* magazine's one-hundred most influential people in the world and received the coveted Julia Child Award.

Owamni is the central point of a 38-acre park project that will also feature Dakota language classes and gardens, complete with placards that explain in both English and Dakota the traditional culinary, nutritional, and medicinal uses of the plants in the park. In addition to the restaurant, Sherman's work includes the Indigenous Food Lab, a nonprofit dedicated to reversing the damage of colonialism and increasing education about Indigenous kitchens all over the United States, producing and selling Indigenous foodstuffs, handicrafts, art, books, and more. Their Instagram page, @indigenousfoodlab, keeps followers apprised of developments, and offers a growing list of North American and Latine Indigenous vendors selling everything from chocolates to hoodies, baby food to books to jewelry, traditional medicines, and herbal teas.

Sherman is a soft-spoken individual with a soothing affect, but whose intensity of purpose is so palpable that it comes across even over the telephone. He described his culinary upbringing to me:

I was born and raised on Pine Ridge, South Dakota, on the Pine Ridge Indian Reservation. Our daily family meals usually consisted of the government commodity food program items. So, lots of canned salmon, canned beef, lots of canned vegetables, lots of powdered milks and government cereals and government cheese, and so forth. We also ate a lot of wild prairie turnips called timpsula. We grew up hunting, so we had a lot of pheasants and grouse and quails and things like that—some venison, some antelopes. And I grew up on a cattle ranch, so we ate a lot of beef.

Sherman's grandparents spoke fluent Lakota and he grew up in a world of tradition. His life's trajectory would take him off the reservation, though, and he quickly discovered his "otherness." Necessity would take him into the world of restaurants and there he rose, becoming the executive chef of several white-tablecloth establishments and corporate cafés by the age of twenty-nine.

But with almost predictable timing, burnout ensued. A recovery sojourn in Mexico allowed Sherman time for rest. With rest came refocusing and, most crucially, Mexico provided an introduction to the Indigenous food and foodways of the Huichol people. This became the catalyst for a reconnection to his own heritage. As he puts it in his cookbook, *The Sioux Chef's Indigenous Kitchen*:

After seeing how the Huicholes held on to so much of their pre-European culture through artwork and food, I recognized that I wanted to know my own food heritage. What did my ancestors eat before the Europeans arrived on our lands? I saw a North America as a whole, with vast and varied landscapes, ancient migrations of people and agriculture whose methods and techniques spread northward with the corn cultures. I saw the deep connections to nature, to the entire ecosystems of the indigenous groups.

The ability to view his own culture from a distant vantage point allowed Sherman to make connections that he had not seen close up, or realized while working in his restaurant life that followed the usual Eurocentric models. In his restaurant world, French and Italian cuisines were king, and "American" cuisine was largely built off of those. But he researched the traditional foods and foodways of the hemisphere's Indigenous people and began to make connections along trade routes that the traditional peoples had maintained for hundreds, if not thousands, of years. Those routes enabled foodways to cross not only modern-day state lines, but national borders as well. North-South trade routes linked communities who had lost or were losing their traditional cultures in the North, with those further south who still vibrantly maintained theirs. There had of course been rich culture and varied foodways here before the Europeans came, and in his travels, Sean was beginning to see them.

He also began to remember his own past and his personal connections to traditional life.

When I first started looking for Indigenous foodways, I was looking for recipes that I could see had a direct connection to the past and weren't influenced by other things too much. I was looking for things that have been very traditional and maintained the same flavors for a long time.

As with many in search of the past, he began with his grandmother.

She seemed to hold on to most of the recipes. My grandfather would bring in some hunted game or take us to harvest some things. But my grandmother would take us out to harvest chokecherries. She would do all of the processing. It was always the women in the kitchen; the women were at the hearth and the men were at the hunt.

Sherman remembered harvesting those chokecherries with her, and the timpsula. He remembered wild potatoes and other tubers that grew and the herbs and grasses that were used. He remembered things like dried chokecherries and herbs and mushrooms being pulverized and used to season meats and vegetables, and began to investigate the range and uses of those ingredients. He remembered wild gingers, wild onions, and wild rice. He especially remembered corn and its central importance. He remembered a diverse pantry of plants and proteins.

Sherman remembered. Then drawing on his chef's training, he began menu planning, reworking, and re-creating. He created a repertoire of recipes that were based in the traditional foods and foodways of his people, but used in innovative and perhaps nontraditional ways.

We're in a modern world today. We have the ability to evolve, but also pay homage and give respect to certain places and people. That's why we set forth challenges for ourselves. . . . How do we create recipes using indigenous ingredients to showcase a modern version of indigenous foods? That is the question I asked. We did our best to remove European and colonial ingredients, so we removed things that didn't exist here for my people just 120 years ago: wheat flour and dairy and cane sugar and beef and pork and chicken. We focused on several questions: What were the regional proteins? What were the regional herbs and plants and ethnobotanical resources? What were the agricultural pieces? What kinds of diversity of corns and beans and squash were being used before European contact? Then, we asked: Do those seeds exist? From that, we worked to create the modern indigenous pantry that we utilize.

The results are evident in the recipes in his book, in the recipes served at Owamni, and the recipes he shared with me here. Dishes like wild rice, formed into savory cakes and baked, served with a sweet-tart berry sauce; and like rabbit, braised with the essence of aromatic maple and spruce. They are dishes that do what Sean Sherman does so well: honor the Indigenous past and place the future firmly on the plate.

BISON AND BUFFALO

While Sean Sherman sings the praises of rabbit as a food source—both for taste and for sustainability—a much larger animal was often the key in many Indigenous diets.

"Oh, give me a home, where the Buffalo roam, and the deer and the antelope play. Where seldom is heard a discouraging word and the skies are not cloudy all day." That idyllic vision of the Plains certainly no longer exists, but the buffalo, also known as bison, is making a comeback.

American bison were the largest land mammal in North America; massive herds of the animals roamed the Plains. Many Native peoples, among them the Lakota, the Shoshone, and the Arapaho, considered the buffalo a sacred animal.

Virtually all parts of the animal were used. Meat could be eaten fresh or dried, or pounded with berries into pemmican, a nutrient- and calorie-rich preserve that could sustain through the harsh winter. Hides became clothing, the hair became headdresses or could be made into rope for use as halters or bridles. The bones were transformed into knives, arrowheads, or awls, and more. The paunch or stomach became portable cooking pots, the skulls were used in ceremonies, and bison horns were carved into bowls. Finally, the dung could be used as fuel.

They were numerous and so valued by the Native peoples that they became pawns in the country's western movement. Because of their importance to the Native peoples, bounties were paid by European settlers for their unbridled slaughter and destruction; they also sought to destroy bison habitat to deprive Natives of this vital food source. By 1900, there were fewer than one thousand buffalo remaining, where once there had been more than fifty million.

By the middle of the twentieth century, there were even fewer. Recently, however, they are again the focus of attention, and there have been attempts at bringing back the buffalo. According to a recent *Washington Post* article,

> Buffalo is the original climate regulator, said Troy Heinert, a member of the Sicangu Lakota (Rosebud Sioux) tribe and executive director of the InterTribal Buffalo Council, a coalition working to restore the animal on tribal lands. "Just by how they use the grass, how they graze, how their hoofs are designed, the way they move. They did this job for us when we allowed them to be buffalo."

Tribes are leading the effort to bring back the bison, Heinert says, which in turn allows for the return of other native grasses, animals, and insects, all of which will "help fight this changing climate." It is ironic indeed that the North American bison that were hunted to almost extinction in the nineteenth century may offer a solution to some of the problems of the twenty-first.

MAPLE AND SPRUCE BRAISED RABBIT
WITH NIXTAMALIZED CORN

SERVES 4 TO 6

The hominy featured in Renée Hunter's Samp (page 40) is featured here in a unique, savory stew of rabbit.

Rabbit was also a common but revered food source across many Indigenous cultures; in a modern preparation, Sean braises rabbit with maple syrup and herbs, including aromatic cedar and spruce, until very tender, pulls it, and pairs the meat and its broth with chewy bites of hominy, garnishing it with fresh wild onions. As Sean says, "Americans should be eating more rabbits because they're all over the place. People get so weird about rabbits. But they're so tasty."

Eastern white cedar and Western red cedar have an edible inner bark. Cedar sprigs for cooking can be obtained from a florist that sells organically grown plants. Be sure to check that you are getting edible cedar, which will give the food a slightly smoky flavor. As for the spruce, all spruce tips are edible, but blue spruce tips have the most flavor. They, like cedar sprigs, are also available from online sources.

3 tablespoons sunflower oil

1 whole rabbit (3 pounds), cut into pieces, like you would a chicken, by the butcher

Kosher salt

3 wild onions or 2 large scallions, coarsely chopped, plus more thinly sliced for garnish

¼ cup maple syrup, or to taste

1 tablespoon finely chopped spruce tips

1 tablespoon finely chopped edible cedar tips

2 carrots, small diced

2 teaspoons dried oregano or wild bergamot (bee balm) leaves

Pinch of ground sumac

1 teaspoon smoked salt

6 cups vegetable stock or water

3 tablespoons corn flour

3 cups cooked hominy (see Note), or 2 (15-ounce) cans, drained and rinsed

1. Preheat the oven to 325°F.

2. In a large Dutch oven, heat the oil over medium heat until it shimmers. Season the rabbit all over with kosher salt, add to the pan, and cook just until lightly browned, turning the pieces over once, about 5 minutes on each side.

3. Around the rabbit, add the onions, maple syrup, spruce tips, cedar tips, carrots, oregano, sumac, and smoked salt. Stir in the stock and corn flour. Reduce the heat to medium-low, cover, and cook until the liquid is simmering.

4. Transfer to the oven and slow-roast until the rabbit is fork-tender, about 2½ hours.

(recipe continues)

5. Carefully transfer the rabbit to a plate. Line a fine-mesh sieve with cheesecloth and set over a large pot. Strain the braising liquid from the Dutch oven through the cheesecloth. Taste and season with more maple syrup and smoked salt as needed.

6. Use two forks to shred the rabbit meat and add it to the strained braising liquid, discarding the bones. Stir in the hominy and cook for 15 to 20 minutes to marry the flavors.

7. Taste and season one more time with smoked salt or maple syrup, as desired. Serve garnished with thinly sliced wild onions.

NOTE: To make hominy from scratch, bring 4 quarts water to a boil and add 2 cups dried field corn and 3 tablespoons baking powder or 1 tablespoon calcium hydroxide. Reduce to a simmer and cook for 2 hours, stirring occasionally and adding more water as needed to keep the corn covered. Drain and rinse the corn extremely well, rubbing off and discarding the hulls. Continue to cook the hominy to desired consistency in more water or soup.

CORN

Corn (*Zea mays*), also called Indian corn or maize, has a long and fascinating history. Corn is native to the Americas and was so central to agriculture in parts of the country that it became a primary deity for many, and was known simply as Mother Corn. The ancestor of today's corn originated about ten thousand years ago as a plant called teosinte, which looked very much like a tall grass and grew in southern Mexico. Through selective planting, Native peoples transformed the plant into what we know today. Slowly, following south-to-north trade routes that had existed for millennia, corn traveled from Mexico into North America where it first appears in Arizona and New Mexico about 4,100 years ago. By 900 CE it was widely adopted in North America, and by the time of European contact, it was found as far north as southern Maine and had become a major staple for many of the Native peoples. It was an early part of the braid, and by 1621 British colonists in the Northeast had grown their first corn crop, thanks to tutelage from the Indians, and grew enough corn to sustain themselves.

The culinary and practical uses of corn seem virtually unlimited. It can be dried and ground into meal or processed and transformed into hominy. The husks can be woven into baskets and mats and even used to make dolls. Finally, the cobs and stocks can be used as fuel. The culinary results range from things like tortillas, to corn breads and pones, to corn oil to popcorn and even alcohols. Corn, with its many uses and deep history, is by far the most widely used cereal in the world today.

WILD RICE

The origin story of the Anishinaabe people, also known as the Chippewa, Ojibwa, and Ojibwe, states that Native peoples originally from the East Coast were given a prophesy: that they would walk to a land where food grows on the water. When they came to what is now known as the northern Midwest, particularly Minnesota, they found wild rice, *Zizania palustris* and *Zizania aquatica,* known in the Ojibwe language as *manoomin,* "the food that grows on water." It is one of the few grains native to North America, and it sustained these communities for centuries; it is impossible to overstate its cultural importance.

Dark in color, firm and satisfying in texture, and nutty and aromatic in flavor, the plant grows in the northern Midwest and southern Canada in shallow water, in small lakes and streams where there is not much current.

Most people are surprised to note that wild rice is in fact not related to domesticated rice.

While domesticated rice is typically grown in paddies and harvested by farmers walking through knee-deep water two or sometimes three times a year, wild rice is traditionally harvested in a very short timeframe in the early fall by taking canoes out into the growing areas. Harvesters carefully bend the plants with ripe grain heads over the canoe, then flail them gently with small paddles, brushing the seeds into the canoe. The freshly harvested grain is then parched, often in iron cauldrons over an open flame. It is then threshed to loosen the outer covering by being danced on in a process called jigging. Finally, the grain is winnowed by tossing it into the air with birchbark trays: The chaff is blown away and the edible grain remains.

All parts of the process are highly regulated because of the grain's centrality to the traditional culture. It is so important that by decree in 2018, the plant was declared sacred and the White Earth Nation of Ojibwe granted wild rice a legal status that is nearly the equivalent of personhood; there are lawsuits to protect its habitat—the "rights of nature"—arguing a revolutionary legal theory that, if effective, can be used as a model to protect ecosystems all over the country.

Wild rice is prepared in a variety of ways ranging from stewing to steaming in porridges both sweet and savory. It can be found from some outlets online, however, it is often truly a case of let the buyer beware as much of what appears in the market commercially as wild rice is not the wild rice of North America at all. Savoring the real thing is a treat indeed, and to do so, be sure to buy it from a Native vendor in person or online.

WILD RICE AND MUSTARD GREEN CAKES
WITH BERRY BERGAMOT SAUCE

SERVES 6

True wild rice is very specific to the Great Lakes region, and pairs well with other flavors from around the Great Lakes, including blueberry, blackberry, and maple sugar.

True wild rice is completely different from the black wild rice that many people are more familiar with. It cooks faster, has a chewy, nutty flavor, and it is really special to the Anishinaabe people of this region; you can purchase it hand-harvested by Indigenous producers. Wild rice is part of the legend of why they wound up here, in Minnesota, whose name means "the place where food grows on top of the water."

The nuttiness of the wild rice blended with the slightly tangy mustard greens and the heartiness of a root vegetable mix that Sean calls an Indigenous mirepoix makes for a surprisingly robust patty.

CAKES

3 cups cooked Minnesota wild rice (see Note), cooled

½ cup finely chopped mix of winter squash, turnip, and sweet potato

2 or 3 large mustard green leaves, stemmed and cut into thin ribbons

¼ cup sunflower oil, plus more as needed

¼ cup maple syrup

1 tablespoon dried or minced fresh sage

Kosher salt

SAUCE

6 cups fresh berries (preferably chokecherries, or a mix)

2 to 3 tablespoons fresh or dried wild bergamot leaves (bee balm; see Note)

¼ cup maple syrup or honey

1. **MAKE THE CAKES:** Preheat the oven to 325°F. Line a baking sheet with parchment.

2. In a food processor, combine the rice and the mix of squash, turnip, and potato, plus the mustard greens, oil, maple syrup, sage, and 1 teaspoon salt. Puree to form a fairly smooth dough. (Add more oil as needed if the dough isn't smooth enough.) Taste and add more salt as needed.

3. Scoop tablespoonfuls of the dough onto the parchment (about 8 cakes) and pat each one into a 6-inch round, leaving about 1 inch between the cakes.

4. Bake until the cakes are firm, 10 to 15 minutes.

5. **MEANWHILE, MAKE THE SAUCE:** In a large saucepan, combine the berries, bergamot, and 1 cup water. Bring to a simmer and cook, stirring occasionally, until the mixture has thickened, 8 to 10 minutes, adding water as needed to keep the mixture syrupy. Sweeten with the maple syrup.

6. Serve the cakes with the sauce for drizzling.

NOTE: To cook the rice, in a medium saucepan, combine 2 cups of Minnesota wild rice with 6 cups of water and bring to a boil over high heat. Reduce heat to a simmer and cook for 45 minutes, covered. If you aren't using true wild rice, and instead have the black wild rice that is actually cultivated, consult the package directions.

NOTE: Wild bergamot in the sauce adds a flavor somewhere between oregano and mint. Be sure you are getting wild bergamot. It's also known as bee balm and is native to North America and not to be confused with the bergamot orange that is grown in Sicily for its oil. Wild bergamot can be foraged, but is also available for purchase online as it is often used as an herbal tea.

THE EUROPEANS

We have mercifully moved beyond the simple glorification of the explorers, settlers, conquistadors, and colonizers who peopled the textbooks of my youth. Our new look at our past has begun to include those who have been excluded from the national narrative and are yet central to it. But of course, it cannot be denied that there is a European thread—and a serious one—running through the history of the country and the foundational food of the United States. However, the Europe these settlers left bore little resemblance to the continent that we know today. In fact, at that time, many of the colonizing countries were only then cementing their own thoughts of nationhood as we know it today.

It is with the arrival of the Europeans that the braiding begins. "First contact" is the term that is now used to designate the initial points of encounter. The Spaniards arrived on the land that would become the continental United States when Ponce de León landed on the shores of Florida in 1513. The ill-fated Roanoke expedition brought the British to these shores in 1584, and then in 1607 with the founding of the Jamestown colony, and the Plymouth colony in 1620. The Dutch rolled into the Hudson in 1609 and the French, late to the game, established Green Bay in 1634. All encountered Native peoples and learned from them.

THE SPANISH

The Spanish arrived in the hemisphere in 1492, one of the few historical dates remembered by most schoolchildren and even the most history-challenged of Americans. What many forget, though, is that the date is doubly notable for Spain, as it also marks the departure of the last Moorish ruler of Granada, Boabdil, and the end of the reconquering of the Iberian Peninsula by the Catholic rulers Ferdinand and Isabella. For seven hundred years prior, the Moors lived and ruled on the Iberian Peninsula, influencing every aspect of Spanish life in Al-Andalus. The Moors also had deep roots on the African continent, and they changed what had been Spanish cuisine by adding to the Spanish larder: rice and myriad rice dishes, olives, almonds and a skill with cooking with nuts and nut pastes, a taste for sweet and sour items, and desserts with Islamic roots, which would be further developed in Iberian convents.

All of this and more would arrive in our land with the Spaniards.

In 1513, Juan Ponce de León arrived in what would become the United States. Later, others followed in search of the Seven Cities of Cíbola reported by the survivors of the doomed mission of Álvar Núñez Cabeza de Vaca, which also brought the first African, Estevanico (aka Mustafa Azemmouri), to the American Southwest. Their tales would inspire Coronado and bring devastation, Spanish rule, and change to what would become the American South and West, from Florida to California. By the time the Spaniards made their first incursions onto the North American continent, they were already developing creolized culinary traditions in Mexico and the Caribbean.

The relatively recent overthrowing of the Moorish rulers in Spain served to embed Roman Catholic traditions even more firmly in the Spanish soul. This was the period of the Spanish Inquisition, during which the consumption of pork became a touchstone, a symbol of adherence to the Roman Catholic faith, and a way of firmly establishing that the swine-eaters were neither Jewish nor Muslim. Catholic Spain had foodways grounded in its own religious traditions that were marked by a calendar of fast days and feast days, many of which had their own traditional foods. These foods and foodways traveled with them, like the sheep and pigs and horses that they brought in their boats from Europe.

In truth, the Spanish who arrived with the aim of colonization and not conquest were in many cases people who had already been "tempered" in Mexico. There, Spanish foodways, already hybridized on the Iberian Peninsula by centuries of Moorish occupation, were further creolized by decades in Mexico, where populations of Spaniards, Native peoples, and Africans mixed and mingled their culinary heritages. There, Spaniards introduced meats like beef, pork, and goat from domesticated animals, and added dairy products and staples like sugar, wheat, and rice to the culinary mix. Complex dishes like mole poblano originated in the monasteries and convents that were also a part of the colonial effort and played a significant role in the development of the New World cuisine. (Note that mole poblano's ingredients include sugar, almonds, and wheat bread.)

THE BRITISH

The history of the British in North America is the one with which we are most familiar: the arrival at Jamestown, Virginia, in 1607 or at Plymouth, Massachusetts, in 1620, followed by contact and "befriending" by the Native peoples. Most have heard of John Smith and Pocahontas in Virginia and the first Thanksgiving in Massachusetts . . . followed by deceptions, broken promises, and the resulting conflicts and confusions that are all too familiar. But we don't really think much of the history of the island nation that began it all. In the mid-seventeenth century, England was undergoing a political upheaval.

King James VI of Scotland ascended to the English throne in 1603 as English King James I. The Gunpowder Plot that was designed to assassinate him and reestablish Catholic rule was revealed in 1605, two years before the founding of the Jamestown colony. The subsequent English Civil War between Catholics and Protestants (cavaliers and roundheads) began in 1642, and the Commonwealths and Protectorates intervened, until the monarchy was reestablished in 1660. This is the world the Pilgrims were fleeing and the one that sent the colonists to Virginia, Massachusetts, and beyond.

For many of us, it is also difficult to think of the early years of the thirteen British colonies that would become the United States as they were in the world at that time. Consider that, from a British perspective, these territories were simply other colonies of a far-flung British empire, an empire where the richest lands were in the more southern Caribbean regions. Barbados in the early decades of the seventeenth century was fast becoming the jewel of the British Empire and that island retains cultural ties with Charleston, South Carolina, to this day. Some Carolina families like the Middletons, the Draytons, and the Bennetts had plantations in both regions. Both the northern colonies and the Caribbean ones were subjects of the same crown and joined by politics and trade. People both free and enslaved—and their foodstuffs—moved back and forth among these sets of colonies.

The England that the colonists left behind was a country deeply divided by class and religion. Those who had patrician roots were used to fine meals of English beef and an abundance of vegetables. Their gardens, tended by others, grew cabbages, broccoli, cucumbers, watercress, turnips, onions, peas, parsnips, and herbs that were popular in English cooking. Peasants were used to another side of the coin and experienced lives of famine and want. They were used to working the soil and were more adaptable to the hardscrabble life that was lived in some of the northern colonies. Pottages and porridges were eaten by all. They were prepared from oats or beans and lentils for the lower classes and thickened with bread. The upper classes also enjoyed pottages; theirs were prepared from wheat and other grains and thickened with jellies and bacon and savories.

The English were fond of ciders, beers, meads, wines, and ales, and all would appear on the newly developing American table. The seventeenth century, though, introduced them to two beverages that would determine the ways of socializing on both sides of the Atlantic for the next centuries: coffee and tea. The two drinks in turn would drive the need for sugar that would lead to the sugar revolution that transformed the agriculture (and the racial structure) of the Caribbean, and firmly established enslavement as the way of the world for the western hemisphere.

THE DUTCH

In the early years of the thirteen colonies, in the lands between the abundant life that was lived in the British Virginia colonies and the more austere British New England colonies, was the colony of New Netherland (*Nieuw Nederland* in Dutch). The Dutch play an interesting role in the creation of American foodways, one where the country's small size is outweighed by its culinary importance.

The Dutch arrived in the New World in 1609 and "discovered" Manhattan Island. First settlements began over a decade later, in 1624. Most schoolchildren know what followed. In 1626, Peter Minuit (director general of the Dutch colony of New Netherland) "purchased" Manhattan Island for what we have been told amounted to $24 in beads and trinkets. In fact, the beads were trade goods that were of use to the Lenape people, who in any case were not "selling" the land, as they had very different ideas of land ownership. Nieuw Amsterdam's uniqueness in the colonial history of what would become the United States comes from its creation. It was not established as a religious refuge, but rather was, in the words of one historian, "a middleman's paradise" devoted to trade. The fledgling colony enjoyed prosperity and boasted a cosmopolitan mix of peoples, including a sizeable proportion of Africans, both free and enslaved, and was a formidable trading hub. In 1664, the English sent a fleet to seize New Netherland, which surrendered with an agreement and without a fight. The colony was renamed New York after the Duke of York, the king's brother, and the Dutch and British went on to live side by side in peace.

The Netherlands that the Dutch had left was a prosperous nation, albeit one that was subject to the religious strife that raged all over Europe. This was a period in which northern Europe came into its own. By the mid-seventeenth century, the nation's trading arm, the Dutch East India Company (Vereenigde Oostindische Compagnie—VOC), was flourishing and bringing vast wealth to the motherland, creating the period known as the Golden Age. Rembrandt was painting and prosperity was expressing itself in Tulipmania: the seventeenth-century speculative bubble in which the traded commodity was tulips.

The seventeenth century was also a culinary Golden Age for the Dutch Republic. The wealthy burghers who are depicted in the paintings of Rembrandt, Vermeer, and Frans Hals consumed varied and luxurious fare like melons, figs, pomegranates, and dates. These were delicacies that made their way to the Netherlands as a result of the Dutch East India Company.

Founded in 1602, the Dutch East India Company is believed to have been one of the largest trading conglomerates to have ever existed. It was a government entity established to form a trading partnership with Mughal India and to aid in the fight for Dutch independence from Spain. (The two countries had been conjoined until the Netherlands declared independence in 1581.) The East India Company also traded with Southeast Asia, over which it held a twenty-one-year monopoly, virtually locking the rest of Europe out of the incredibly lucrative spice trade. As a result of the company, the Netherlands was involved with the importation of spices as well as coffee and tea to Europe. Exotic ingredients, like dates, ginger, saffron, spices, wines, cheeses, and nuts, were readily available to the wealthy Dutch burghers of Amsterdam, the major port for the Dutch East India Company and throughout the Low Countries.

Originally brought by the Spaniards, but popularized by the British and the Dutch, coffee from the East began to show up on the tables of the wealthy. By the seventeenth century, the consumption of tea and coffee was a part of everyday life for the well-to-do. The still-life paintings of the times by artists like Clara Peeters and Pieter Claesz that show arrays of cheeses and breads baked with white wheat flour as well as olives and lemons give a sense of the culinary range indulged in by the upper classes. This is the abundance that would have turned up on the tables of the good burghers in New Netherland—and later New York—that are the subjects of Washington Irving's tales.

THE FRENCH

France, the most populous country in Europe in the seventeenth century, was dominated by three rulers: Henri IV, Louis XIII, and the Sun King, Louis XIV. Although Henri IV was a Protestant himself who converted to Catholicism to attain the throne, during this time Protestants were persecuted and many emigrated to the New World.

The French who initially arrived in the North American part of the hemisphere were explorers who came in the sixteenth century in search of a route to Asia, and wealth. Several small and unsuccessful settlements were established, but it was only in 1634 that Jean Nicolet founded what would become today's Green Bay, Wisconsin. By the end of the seventeenth century, other settlements had been created and René-Robert Cavelier, Sieur de La Salle established a network of forts from the Great Lakes to the Gulf of Mexico. The first capital of French La Louisiane was established near what is today Mobile, Alabama, in 1702 and Jean-Baptiste le Moyne, Sieur de Bienville founded La Nouvelle-Orléans in 1718.

The French who initially came were traders and explorers and there were few women. Unlike the Spanish, British, or Dutch, many French men formed relationships with and married Native peoples. Under the rule of Louis XIV, eight hundred women were sent out to the colonies and called the King's Daughters, but the population of New France remained low. In 1663, the population of New France was only twenty-five hundred and in 1718 there were only seven hundred Europeans in Louisiana. Convicts and prostitutes were among those who were sent to the New World between 1719 and 1721 until the good folk who had emigrated complained about the class of people being sent.

The large swath of territory that represented New France and the diversity of the population meant that the French foodways that arrived in the hemisphere were varied indeed. Those who were aligned with the original explorers and those who emigrated under the king's auspices would have been accustomed to a different level of fare than those who were the former convicts and prostitutes.

The French fare consumed in American restaurants today in the first quarter of the twenty-first century bears little resemblance to the foods that were actually eaten in New France, or in France itself. In France in the eighteenth century, at the upper level, people would have been accustomed to some of the foods codified by François Pierre de la Varenne in 1631 when he wrote *Le Cuisinier François*, an attempt to gallicize the French food that he deemed too Italian—indeed, the Queen of France in the latter half of the sixteenth century was a Florentine, born Caterina de' Medici. She is credited with having brought the fork into French culture. In la Varenne's cuisine, though, pepper, saffron, cinnamon, ginger, and cloves were used in the creation of dishes like bouillons, bisques, omelets, and more that were designed to satisfy the eye as well as the palate. If meat had primacy of place in the early part of the century, by the second half, vegetables grew in importance. The growing bourgeoisie consumed meals that mirrored those of the aristocracy but in lesser quantity, with fewer courses and less elaborate preparations. The poor, as they had in the rest of Europe, subsisted on pottages and coarse breads; in France the rustic dishes were washed down by coarse wines. Chowders were developed as were pot pies, some even using New World ingredients like turkey, and, with the French adopting New World haricot beans, dishes like cassoulet became some of the regional mainstays of French cooking. These then, were the foods—simple and complex—that would journey to the French tables of the New World.

The early Europeans left a massive mark on our national foodways; they introduced foodstuffs and animals that have become American staples. Where would Johnny Appleseed be without European apples? Where would North Carolina barbecue be without the Spanish-introduced pig? Europeans colonized the foods of the Native peoples and appropriated methods and foodstuffs like the native turkey and Corn Mother, but they also gave the cooking of what would become the United States wheat and honeybees, sheep and cattle.

In this chapter, I look to stories and heritage European recipes from far-flung corners of the country. In the Texas borderlands, an eighth-generation Texan and descendant of the Spanish in that region, Melissa Guerra, conjoins Spanish salt cod, a staple on sailing ships, and traditional Mexican seasonings and culinary techniques in turnovers called empanadas de bacalao. In Charleston, South Carolina, Kit Bennett celebrates the roasting traditions of England with a leg of lamb, but also acknowledges the influence of the African hand in the cooking of her hometown with okra soup and red rice: dishes that may have first been seen in Barbados by her British ancestors who lived there in the seventeenth century before migrating to Charleston, following a pattern evidenced by many of South Carolina's early setters. Peter Rose reminds us all not to forget the Dutch, whose gifts to the American culinary repertoire include waffles and cookies and even coleslaw, while in Louisiana, Louis Costa celebrated his connection to his French ancestry with a multigenerational catalogue of recipes, many of them for the celebrations that his New Orleans hometown holds so dear.

All point to the important contributions that the European thread of the braid brought, but also remind us of the multiple ways in which European cuisines began to mix and comingle with those of other nations very early on in the culinary history of that continent.

DAUGHTER OF THE WILD HORSE DESERT

MELISSA GUERRA

It's hard to miss Melissa Guerra in a crowd; she's a jeans-wearing, 5-foot 10-inch redhead who is a force of nature. I first met her when we were both on the advisory board for the Culinary Institute of America's campus in San Antonio. We'd been distant acquaintances for more than a decade, but it was only when another Texas friend suggested that I speak with her about her deep Spanish origins that we really bonded over food history. I knew that she was a Texan—that's clear the moment you meet her—but I had no idea of the depths of her Texas roots. She explains:

My grandfather's name was Argyle McAllen, but his first language was Spanish. My family has been here since I think around 1743, a very long time. I'm an eighth-generation Texan. My ancestors arrived with the Spanish, one of the original Spanish families that came over to the New World and got a land grant. Eventually the Spanish name morphed into a Scotch Irish name. In fact, John McAllen, the settler whose ranch became the town site of McAllen, Texas, was my great-great-grandfather.

The area I live in is 95 percent Hispanic, 75 percent Spanish speaking. It is a point between where English ends and Spanish begins. I moved away for a few years and then got to know my husband and came back to the border. I was born here, and I just don't wanna be anyplace else.

Anyone who has read the novel *Like Water for Chocolate* by Laura Esquivel understands something about the complexity of the Norteño border culture, and the porosity of the border, in the first two-thirds of the twentieth century. The novel paints a vivid picture of the rich and complicated life of the borderlands that Melissa calls the Wild Horse Desert.

Today, Melissa's Wild Horse Desert is at the epicenter of the current and oh-so-very real political conflict about the border between the US and Mexico, with walls going up and once free-flowing crossing spots now firmly closed. It was not always thus.

Back in the day when we were young, my husband and me, we would just go back and forth across the border. No big deal. You know, go to Mexico for lunch, come back to the office: back and forth, back and forth. It really didn't have anything to do with people jockeying for citizenship or anything. Ranching families back in the day would just go back and forth across the border. . . .

The historic ease of crossing the border, and the resulting ebb and flow of ideas and people, led to a blending of cultures that produced a world of its own.

I live here on the border of Texas; it's very unfamiliar territory and I figure I need everything in my arsenal to communicate who we are, what we do, why we do it, and why you should come down. Because we are awesome.

Melissa is a writer and a food blogger who writes about food and also takes photographs, because, as she puts it, "I live at a dovetail place."

The convoluted complexity of life on the border is what began to get Melissa interested in food history. Her curiosity about the food and foodways of her region was further piqued after her marriage. "My husband was born in the same hospital that I was. We were delivered by the same doctor. At different times and from different mothers, of course," she jokes.

We were both born on the US side, but his family had a ranch in Mexico. So that's where they always lived. Once I got married, I was exposed to completely different interpretations of our local foods. It was the same food; it was just cooked differently. . . . My husband's family, for example is very anti-cumin; my family was very pro cumin. In some cases, it's as basic as that.

On my family's ranch back in the day, there were a lot of cowboys. There was a camp cook, and he would prepare flour tortillas for all of the guys in the morning, and then my family would come and get some. It was refried beans and tortillas every day and every meal with the exception of breakfast because, in the 1960s, it was all

about Kellogg breakfast cereals and I was into Tony the Tiger, but lunch and dinner was always beans and tortillas.

Rice was a bigger deal in my husband's family; they had rice every meal. We would sometimes have corn tortillas for dinner because they are more savory.

Rice is especially telling as an ingredient beloved in her husband's family, for it is a profound culinary connector between the former Spanish territories and Spain—think paella Valenciana. Even more interesting and further complicating the American braid, it connects Spain to Africa via the North African Moors, who originally brought rice to Spain. In fact, Melissa's family's participation in America's celebrated cowboy culture acknowledges that it owes much to the Spaniards—after all it would not exist as we know it without the horses and the cattle that they brought.

Melissa's study of the food and foodways of her region has led her to research varying aspects of its food. She has examined the importance of pit cooking, calling the hole in which the food is cooked, "the biggest, cheapest clay pot that a human being could come up with." She reminds us all of the importance of mesquite, the hot hardwood with a greasy smoke, that was used for not only for cooking, but everything:

Mesquite was our only fuel and our only wood. The way it proliferated was through the cattle industry, but it was used not only to cook; the coal would go into your iron for clothes; the fuel that would teach your house every aspect of heat and energy that was available to people who didn't have a lot of resources. Mesquite wood is absolutely pervasive—it's primordial; it's essential.

With an eye simultaneously on the past and a look toward the future, she is especially interested in water use and water sovereignty, and its importance as a parallel study to that of colonization. Water sources have historically been sites for the establishment of cities and civilizations, and as we are all beginning to now know, will be a defining question of humankind's future survival. For Melissa, this knowledge is at the core of the civilization of her beloved valley.

> *Colonizers wanted to appropriate whatever the Indigenous had already developed. That includes not only the watering holes, but access to the underground aquifers and riverside property that would then be used for irrigating croplands. The presence of water makes the Rio Grande Valley where I live incredibly interesting. . . . My area is still called the Magic Valley because you could grow crops, dryland crops; we have everything from sugarcane to citrus, cotton, sorghum, as well as the cattle ranches for which the area is known.*

Where some people may see desert on a map, Melissa understands it to be a place of rich food and agriculture—and therefore of culture. And understanding its past as a colonized place, and its present as a place of symbolic and real political conflict, she knows that nothing about her place is permanent. It is, as she says, a dovetail place; a joint, and places that need joinery inevitably mean tension and change. Melissa is a crusader, one who is at the forefront of documenting her community's culinary culture and keeping it alive. Recognizing the ephemeral nature of many traditional food cultures, and given the added difficulty of living on a border that is increasingly under stress, she has undertaken the heroic task of telling the world about the uniqueness of her Wild Horse Desert and of the culinary diversity of the Norteño culture that is the hyphen between Mexico and the United States of America.

STEWED SALT COD IN TOMATO SAUCE
BACALAO

SERVES 4 TO 6

While fish is not necessarily the first thing that comes to mind when thinking of the cuisine of the Southwest or Texas, bacalao, or salt cod, is an ingredient that speaks to the Spanish influences on the Norteño kitchen. In Spain, dishes prepared from the salted fish are traditionally eaten during Lent and the Holy Week period leading up to Easter, when eating meat was forbidden by the Roman Catholic church. More important, salt cod was also easily transportable. It became a mainstay of cooking on ocean voyages, and as such became an important part of New World cooking.

This savory stew of firm, umami-laden salt cod in tomato sauce with olives and capers can be eaten as a main dish, or used to fill delicate turnovers known as empanadas de bacalao (see Note on page 87).

1 pound bacalao (salt cod)

¼ cup olive oil

2 tablespoons minced onion

1 pound tomatoes, peeled, seeded, and chopped

½ red bell pepper, finely chopped

1 tablespoon minced fresh parsley

2 tablespoons capers, rinsed

½ cup chopped pitted green olives

1. In a colander, rinse the bacalao under running water, scrubbing to remove excess salt. In a large bowl, cover the bacalao with cool water and soak overnight in the refrigerator.

2. Drain and rinse the bacalao again. Place it in a 12-inch skillet and cover with fresh water. Bring to a simmer over medium-high heat, then reduce the heat to low and cook gently for 10 to 15 minutes. Taste the bacalao to make sure the flavor is not too salty; if it is, add an additional cup of water and cook for 10 minutes more. Transfer the bacalao to a plate and discard the water.

3. Rinse and dry the skillet. Add the oil to the skillet and heat over medium heat until shimmering. Add the onion, tomatoes, bell pepper, and parsley and sauté until the tomatoes have dissolved into a pulp, about 10 minutes. Continue cooking, stirring occasionally, until there is no more freestanding liquid in the pan.

4. Add 1 cup water, the bacalao, capers, and olives. Cover, reduce the heat to medium-low, and simmer for 20 minutes, breaking the bacalao into flakes with the back of a wooden spoon as it cooks.

5. Uncover and continue to cook until the liquid has reduced to a thick sauce, about 10 minutes. Serve immediately.

NOTE: To make empanadas de bacalao, place 2 tablespoons of chilled Stewed Salt Cod in Tomato Sauce (page 85) in the center of a store-bought puff pastry round. Fold the round to form a half-moon and use your hands to pinch or a fork to seal the edges. Repeat with the remaining puff pastry. Bake at 375°F until golden brown, 20 to 25 minutes.

ENCHILADAS SUIZAS

SERVES 8 TO 10

The practice of wrapping a tortilla around ingredients dates to Aztec times, but enchiladas suizas only go back to the 1950s when they were first served at a Sanborns café, a coffee shop chain in Mexico City. The suiza part comes from the use of dairy in the dish, as dairies were developed in Mexico by Swiss immigrants (*suiza* means "Swiss" in Spanish). Filled with melted cheese and chicken, the enchiladas are baked with a brightly flavored tomatillo salsa, making for a rich but balanced dish that is a perfect combining of the creaminess of the cheesy chicken stuffing enlivened by the sharp punctuation of the salsa.

SAUCE

2 pounds fresh tomatillos, husked and rinsed well

2 tablespoons olive oil

1 small yellow onion, chopped

1 or 2 garlic cloves, minced

Kosher salt and freshly ground black pepper

TO ASSEMBLE

16 to 24 (6-inch) corn tortillas

4 ounces white cheese, such as Monterey Jack, grated

4 ounces queso fresco, crumbled

FILLING

2 tablespoons olive oil

1 small yellow onion, chopped

8 ounces cream cheese

1 pound shredded cooked chicken (a rotisserie bird is great for this)

Kosher salt and freshly ground black pepper

¼ cup Mexican crema or sour cream

Chopped fresh cilantro, for garnish

1. **MAKE THE SAUCE:** In a large saucepan, combine the tomatillos with enough water to cover by 1 to 2 inches Bring to a boil over high heat and cook for 5 minutes. Drain, discarding the water. Transfer the tomatillos to a blender and puree; it doesn't have to be totally smooth.

2. In a large skillet, heat the oil over medium heat until shimmering. Add the onion and sauté until translucent, about 2 minutes. Add the garlic and sauté for about 10 seconds. Pour in the pureed tomatillos and season with salt and pepper to taste. Cook for 2 minutes just to marry the flavors, then remove from the heat.

3. **MAKE THE FILLING:** In a large skillet, heat the oil over medium heat until shimmering. Add the onion and sauté until translucent, about 3 minutes. Add the cream cheese, stirring until it has melted. Stir in the cooked chicken. Season with salt and pepper to taste.

4. Preheat the oven to 350°F.

5. **TO ASSEMBLE:** Stack and wrap the tortillas in a clean, damp kitchen towel and heat them in the microwave for a minute or so, until pliable.

6. Divide the filling equally among the warm tortillas, roll them up, and arrange in one or two large casserole dishes. Pour the tomatillo sauce evenly over the top of the enchiladas, top with the grated white cheese, and cover the casserole(s) loosely with aluminum foil.

7. Bake until the enchiladas are bubbling and the cheese has melted, about 15 minutes.

8. Uncover and top with the crumbled queso fresco, Mexican crema, and some cilantro. Serve immediately.

TEXAS CHILE CON CARNE

SERVES 12

The number or arguments that have been had about chile con carne are legion and range from how it is spelled (chili, chilli, chille, or chile), to whether or not it should include beans. Eighth-generation Texan Melissa Guerra's recipe goes under the title of chile con carne—using the Spanish spelling—and yes, she uses beans, arguing that the Chile Queens of San Antonio, who hawked their wares near the Alamo, probably would have added beans to their dish in order to stretch their recipe and add to their profits.

The Chile Queens of San Antonio were a formidable group of Mexican cooks who set up tables and cook stalls and created what amounted to pop-up Mexican restaurants on Market Square beginning in the 1880s. They are credited with popularizing the border food that we now call Tex-Mex food. However, by the 1940s, because of hygiene issues and growing racism toward the Mexican women, the Chile Queens were no more.

Although this recipe is not very spicy, you can always add more chipotle for heat. If you can't find dried chipotles, you can substitute canned chipotles in adobo sauce. Three canned chiles equate to the same heat level as ½ ounce of dried chipotle chiles.

Chile con carne is best when prepared 24 hours in advance, refrigerated, and reheated to serve. The resting time allows the flavors to marry more completely. This recipe can easily be doubled to feed more people, or cut in half to feed fewer.

½ ounce dried chipotle chiles

2 ounces dried ancho chiles

2 ounces dried guajillo or pasilla chiles

2 large garlic cloves, peeled but whole

1 pound tomatoes, peeled, seeded, and coarsely chopped

2 tablespoons olive oil

1 pound white onions, coarsely chopped

3 pounds coarsely ground beef

2 pounds coarsely ground pork

1 tablespoon kosher salt, plus more to taste

1½ cups cooked kidney beans or 1 (15-ounce) can, drained and rinsed (optional)

GARNISHES

Grated cheddar or crumbled Cotija cheese

Chopped fresh cilantro

Chopped white onions

Avocado slices

(recipe continues)

1. In a medium saucepan, combine all of the dried chiles with enough cold water to come halfway up the sides of the pan. Bring to a boil over medium heat. Reduce the heat to medium-low and simmer until the chiles are tender, about 5 minutes. Cool slightly, then drain, discarding the liquid.

2. Discard the stems and seeds of the chiles, rinsing the chiles under running water briefly to remove any remaining seeds.

3. In a blender, combine the seeded chiles, garlic, and chopped tomatoes. Add 1 cup water and puree until smooth. Add more water if needed to facilitate blending.

4. In a large Dutch oven, heat the oil over medium heat until shimmering. Add the onions and sauté until they brown around the edges, 7 to 10 minutes.

5. Increase the heat to high. Add the ground beef and pork and cook until the meat is browned, stirring occasionally, about 15 minutes. Use a wooden spoon to break up the ground meats.

6. Stir in the pureed chile mixture and the salt and bring to a simmer. Reduce the heat to medium-low, cover, and simmer until the meat is tender, about 30 minutes, stirring occasionally to avoid any scorching.

7. Add the beans, if desired, and cook for 5 minutes more, until they are heated through. Taste and adjust the seasoning with salt.

8. Serve hot, topped with any or all of the garnishes.

COWBOYS AND CATTLE RANCHERS

It is difficult to envision the capacity of the ships that made the original crossings from Europe to the Americas. They were very small indeed. I think of them as almost like walnut shells tossed into the sea. The interesting fact is that they could and did accommodate a surprising number of passengers. Not only were there the human passengers, but there were also livestock, provisions, and seeds; all designed to not only sustain the travelers during their voyage, but also allow them to have a start in the new lands to which they were bound.

In this manner, animals made the transatlantic crossings, arriving as early as with Columbus, and continuing through to the journeys of the original European settlers and beyond. Pigs (see Pigs "R" Us, page 96) were useful as they provided meat and consumed garbage. Chickens not only gave eggs but could serve as the occasional Sunday dinner on the voyages that could last weeks if not months, and cows gave milk.

Domestic cattle arrived with Columbus on his second voyage in 1493 and they were rapidly transported throughout southern North America. In the Caribbean region, they reproduced so well and so quickly that by 1512 it was no longer necessary to import cattle into the region. They were introduced into Mexico in 1521 and moved north, mixing with other breeds imported into the fledgling country from northern Europe, and becoming the ancestors of the Texas longhorn cattle that were for centuries the predominant American breed.

According to some scholars, elevated disease resistance of Texas longhorn cattle (compared with the northern European cattle breeds that had been imported to southwestern North America) may be partially related to the portions of their genomes that stem from African ancestry. Their descendants are also known for their ability to withstand droughts better than their European counterparts.

Travelers in the 1700s in the region that is now Texas signaled the presence of wild cattle that were erroneously thought to be native. The herds of Texas longhorn cattle roamed a wide area from the Red River to the Rio Grande east to Louisiana and west to the upper Brazos River. They continued to roam wild until the end of the Civil War.

After the Civil War, they began to be herded, rounded up, and driven up various trails from Texas to Kansas City to be put on trains to the northern and eastern slaughterhouses. This herding and transporting required skilled individuals who were adept at riding, roping, and generally watching over the herds on the trails. The men who excelled at the tasks became the American cowboys. (And fully one-third of them were African American!) Estimates suggest that between 1867 and 1880 nearly ten million head of cattle were driven north along the trails to market, and the United States became a nation of beef eaters.

GREEN CHILI
CHILE VERDE
SERVES 6

While this chili is eaten all over the Southwest, it is more typical of the Santa Fe area. This recipe calls for cubed meat rather than ground meat, which adds a silkier taste to the chili.

The beef and pork used in this recipe are both gifts to the American table from the Spaniards. Pigs and beef cattle arrived with Europeans early on and transformed the foodways of all. Pigs arrived with Hernando de Soto, who brought them from Europe for food for the journey of conquest. Pigs being pigs, they either escaped, went free range, or were abandoned. The result of this was an incredible population of wild swine throughout the southeastern United States. Their feral descendants still survive, and are currently a problem for many communities because they are destroying farmlands and the levees that contain the Mississippi River.

Beef cattle arrived in Vera Cruz, Mexico, in the early sixteenth century and became a part of the Spanish march northward. The early arrival of beef cattle again evidences a further confusing of the American braid in the case of the Spaniards, as many of the foodways they brought with them had already been interwoven with those of the African continent from seven hundred years of occupation by the Moors.

Most are usually astounded to learn that the Texas longhorn cattle that were the foundation of the beef industry, have DNA from the Fulani cattle of Western Africa via the bloodstock of Iberian cattle. In Melissa Guerra's Wild Horse Desert of Texas, it's a complex braid indeed.

- 2 pounds bone-in pork chops
- 2 tablespoons vegetable oil
- 1 medium yellow onion, finely chopped
- 1½ pounds cubed beef stew meat
- 3 garlic cloves, minced
- ½ cup chopped fresh parsley
- 1 (20-ounce) can hot or mild Hatch green chile peppers, drained
- 1 (28-ounce) can tomatillos, drained or 1½ pounds fresh, husked and boiled
- ¼ teaspoon ground cloves
- 1 teaspoon ground cumin
- ¼ cup fresh lime juice
- Kosher salt and freshly ground black pepper
- Crumbled queso fresco, for serving
- Tortilla chips, for serving

1. Cut the meat away from the bones. Reserve the bones. Cut the pork into bite-sized pieces.

2. In a Dutch oven, heat the oil over medium-high heat until shimmering. Add the onion and sauté until translucent, about 3 minutes.

3. Push the onions to one side of the pot and add the pork, bones, and beef cubes in one layer. Cook, turning occasionally, until well browned, about 4 minutes. (Do this in batches to avoid overcrowding.) Add the garlic and parsley and cook for about 30 seconds.

4. Add the canned chiles, tomatillos, cloves, cumin, and lime juice. Use a wooden spoon to stir while breaking up the tomatillos.

5. Season with salt and pepper, cover, reduce the heat to medium-low, and simmer until the meats are tender, about 2 hours. Keep an eye on the liquid level, adding up to 2 cups water, as needed to maintain a thin stew.

6. Season with salt and pepper and remove the pork bones. Serve hot with the queso fresco and chips.

PIGS "R" US

While many think only of the botanical aspect of the ebb and flow of foodstuffs between the old world of Europe (and beyond) and the Americas that is often referred to as the Columbian Exchange, there was equally a zoological component. Along with the transfer of chiles, tomatoes, potatoes, and chocolate from the New World to the Old, horses, goats, sheep, cattle, and pigs arrived from Europe, made themselves at home in the Americas, transformed the lifestyles of the nascent nation, and gradually became emblematic of its food and its cultures.

Horses and cattle found their way north and west from Mexico; sheep, in managed flocks, became mainstays of tribes in places like New Mexico; and pigs, being pigs, went feral and took over.

Eight pigs sailed with Columbus on his second voyage. Hernando de Soto brought them to what would become the United States, landing in Tampa Bay in 1539 with thirteen of them in cargo. Pigs are hardy animals and have the advantage of being willing to eat almost anything, and so could survive the lengthy ocean voyages without requiring much upkeep. In addition, almost everything on the pig could be eaten or transformed into something useful. They multiplied and by the time of de Soto's death, there were seven hundred of them. Hernán Cortés brought swine to New Mexico in 1600 and Sir Walter Raleigh brought sows to the Jamestown colony in 1607. Their descendants show up on the table as everything from baked Virginia ham to bacon, from pork chops to sausage meat, to hog's head cheese to pigs' feet. And what would barbecue be without spareribs, smoked butt, and whole hogs?

But all is not simple pleasure in the American world of pigs. Pigs seem to be the gift that got out of hand. Many of the original pigs escaped and became the ancestors of today's feral swine, also known as wild boars, that now are numbered as six million strong. They create havoc in thirty-five states where they do untold damage to levees, destroy crops, uproot landscapes, and spread disease. The US Department of Agriculture has even got a campaign entitled "Manage the Damage" designed to control them. Some parts of Texas offer a bounty for each wild pig tail turned in by a licensed hunter. The good news is that if proper precautions are taken by hunters when the hogs are killed, they are safe for human consumption, and according to those who have sampled them, they make pretty good eating indeed.

GREEN CHILI ENCHILADAS

SERVES 8

Melissa stresses the fact that in the American Southwest there are almost as many chili recipes as there are grandmothers. The varieties are seemingly endless. Melissa offered this recipe to give a feeling for the range of recipes and also to salute the Spanish influences on the American braid that range far beyond her Wild Horse Desert. While the Green Chili (Chile Verde; see page 95) is a meaty stew, whose richness is attenuated by tart-sweet tomatillos and the complex flavor of green chiles, these enchiladas feature a variant of New Mexico's Santa Fe chili verde.

Much more of a sauce than a stew, it's a pure expression of the flavor of charred chiles, accompanied only by onion and thickened with corn. Its richness comes in the form of a generous filling of cheese, baked until molten and married to the flavor of chiles.

And while we're discussing comparisons and contrasts, this enchilada may look similar to the Enchiladas Suizas (page 88), but it is *very* different in taste and gustatorily demonstrates the vast and complex range of enchiladas with variants that are not only regional but often also familial.

1 pound fresh green Anaheim or Hatch chile peppers

2 tablespoons vegetable oil

1 small onion, cut into ¼-inch dice

1 garlic clove, minced

1 tablespoon masa harina (corn tortilla mix)

Kosher salt and freshly ground black pepper

16 (6-inch) corn tortillas

1 pound Monterey Jack cheese, grated

½ cup Mexican crema or sour cream, for garnish

Chopped fresh cilantro, for garnish

1. Char the chiles over an open flame or under a broiler, turning until they are blackened all over. Wrap them in a clean kitchen towel or in a paper bag. Wait 15 minutes, then scrape off the charred skins. Stem and seed the chiles, rinse to remove excess skin or seeds, and coarsely chop.

2. In a sauté pan, heat the oil over medium heat until shimmering. Add the onion and garlic and sauté until translucent, 7 to 10 minutes. Stir in the masa harina until all of the oil is absorbed.

3. Stir in 1 cup water until well incorporated. When the mixture is thickened and bubbling, add the chopped chiles. Season with salt and pepper, cover, reduce the heat to medium-low, and simmer for 10 minutes to form a thick sauce.

4. Preheat the oven to 350°F. Line one or two 9 × 13-inch ceramic or metal baking pans with parchment paper. (You may need to use only one baking dish, depending on how tightly you roll or pack the enchiladas.)

5. Stack and wrap the tortillas in a clean, damp kitchen towel and heat them in the microwave for a minute or so, until pliable (or you can heat the tortillas individually on a griddle).

6. Place 2¾ tablespoons of the grated cheese on each tortilla, roll them up, and arrange them in a single layer, seam-sides down in the baking dishes. Pour the green chile sauce over the enchiladas and scatter the remaining grated cheese over the top. Cover the baking dish(es) tightly with aluminum foil.

7. Bake until all the cheese has melted and the sauce is bubbling, about 25 minutes.

8. To serve, uncover and spoon or drizzle the Mexican crema over the enchiladas and top with the cilantro.

ROASTED ONION AND TOMATO SALSA

MAKES ABOUT 2 CUPS

According to Melissa, "giving a salsa recipe is like giving a recipe for a sandwich." There are myriad different variations, and ultimately what matters is what the cook wants it to taste like in the end. Ingredients are dependent on individual taste preferences and more. Still, a personal, go-to, go-with-anything salsa is a must for any cook, and this one has worked for Melissa. It showcases New World tomatoes and hot chiles, and Old World onions that are thought to have originated in Central Asia, and brings them together by first charring them for smoky complexity, then blending and stewing them briefly to concentrate the flavor.

3 tablespoons olive oil

1 small white onion, halved

1 pound tomatoes

4 serrano chile peppers

Kosher salt and freshly ground black pepper

1. Brush the surface of a griddle or large cast-iron skillet with 1 tablespoon of the oil and heat over medium-high heat until very hot, but not quite smoking.

2. Working in batches, sear the onion, tomatoes, and chiles until the chile skins blister and blacken all over. You will need to turn the peppers and tomatoes to roast on all sides, but the onion halves can remain face down.

3. Discard any stems and transfer the blackened vegetables to a blender or food processor. Pulse or blend just until chunky, being careful not to break them down too much. (The salsa should have texture.)

4. In a small skillet, heat the remaining 2 tablespoons oil over low heat. Pour the salsa into the oil and cook until its juices have almost reduced entirely, 10 to 15 minutes.

5. Taste and season with salt and pepper. Transfer to a container to cool for 10 minutes, then cover and refrigerate for at least 1 hour before serving.

WHEAT: AMBER WAVES OF GRAIN

Wheat, the name for the many species that make up the *Triticum* genus, was probably first cultivated in the Fertile Crescent in the modern-day Middle East around 9600 BCE. From there, it spread to Europe where wheat bread became popular. By the eighteenth century, loaves of fluffy wheat breads became a sign of affluence, supplanting the barley, oats, and rye that had previously been the more accessible and popular grains.

The Spaniards brought wheat to the New World in the 1500s, and it was probably first cultivated in Ecuador. Eventually, it spread to the American Southwest via Spanish settlers in Mexico. Other explorers and colonizers brought it to the eastern US, where it was grown as one of the main cash crops during the Colonial era. Back then, it was sown by casting it to the wind, reaped with sickles, threshed by flails, and taken to gristmills for processing. Among the practitioners of this was George Washington's estate at Mount Vernon.

Wheat breads and cakes retained their aristocratic standing because as late as 1830, it took four people, working with two oxen, ten hours to produce two hundred bushels. It was only with the advent of new wheat cultivars and new agricultural technology that wheat become a major American cash crop. Today, wheat yields almost twice as much grain per acre as barley and more than twice as much as oats; it is only surpassed by corn. America is ranked fourth in world production of wheat, with fifty million tons of the grain produced in 2020, and the amber waves of grain wave on.

TRADITIONAL CINNAMON SHORTBREAD COOKIES
PAN DE POLVO

MAKES 72 COOKIES

Not to overstate the importance of the almighty pig in colonial Spanish foodways, but note that these addictive shortbread cookies are prepared with lard. Aside from that beloved fat, there are only very simple ingredients: really just flour (itself at one time a prestige ingredient; see "Wheat: Amber Waves of Grain," page 99) and maybe some pecans with a little bit of sugar and cinnamon. Melissa says, "They just melt in your mouth. They're really, really incredibly delicious. We cannot have Christmas without them; you absolutely have to have them."

While the pan de polvo cookies are essential in Melissa's celebration, many people do not understand why they are traditionally Christmas cookies. Melissa explained that the cooler weather around Christmas was the time of hog killing—less heat means the pork has more of a chance of preservation before spoilage—and with the processing of the hog, freshly rendered lard would be available for the cookies.

1 or 2 (3-inch)
  cinnamon sticks
5 to 6 cups all-purpose
  flour, plus more
  dusting
1¼ cups sugar
1 tablespoon ground
  cinnamon

1½ teaspoons baking
  powder
2¾ cups lard
  or vegetable
  shortening

FOR COATING
1½ cups sugar

1 tablespoon ground
  cinnamon

1. In a small saucepan, combine 2 cups water and 1 cinnamon stick (or 2 sticks for more cinnamon flavor). Bring to a boil over medium-high heat and cook for 4 minutes. Remove from the heat to steep and cool to room temperature. Discard the cinnamon stick(s). Set the cinnamon "tea" aside.

2. Preheat the oven to 350°F. Line several baking sheets with parchment paper.

3. In a stand mixer fitted with the paddle, combine 5 cups of the flour, the sugar, ground cinnamon, baking powder, and lard and mix on low speed. Add ¾ cup of the cinnamon tea and beat until a smooth dough forms, adding more liquid as needed. Discard the excess tea.

4. Lightly flour a clean work surface and dump the dough onto it. Use some or all of the remaining 1 cup flour to hand knead into the dough. The dough should be soft but not sticky.

5. Reflour the work surface and roll out the dough to a ¼-inch thickness. Use a 2-inch round cookie cutter to cut the cookies. Gather the scraps and reroll the dough as needed. Arrange the cookies on the baking sheets, spacing the cookies 1 inch apart.

6. Bake one sheet at a time until golden, 10 to 12 minutes.

7. **MEANWHILE, MAKE THE COATING:** In a shallow bowl, mix the sugar and cinnamon.

8. Cool the cookies briefly on the baking sheet. While they are warm, transfer a few at a time to the cinnamon sugar to coat on both sides.

9. Cool completely and keep in an airtight container at room temperature.

THE NOTORIOUS K.I.T.

KIT BENNETT

Charleston, South Carolina, is an old place, rife with traditions and complex with social ins and outs that are as circuitous as some of the city's alleyways. I met Kit Bennett there more than twenty-five years ago. We were introduced by a friend, Mitchell Crosby, who thought her house would be the perfect spot for a gathering for *Garden Design* magazine, which I was asked to host. It was. A glorious Charleston single house in a prestigious neighborhood, it totally fit the desired patrician profile; it looked for all the world like the home of a daughter of a British colonial family that it was. Kit's ancestors go back to Charleston's beginnings; the crumbling facade of the Bennett rice mill remains a fixture of the city. However, when Kit came down the stairs to meet me, she was wearing an Indian sari. I figured she was going to be different.

And I knew it, when I asked her how long she'd been in Charleston. "Since dirt," she replied. Then, when asked to tell me a bit about Charleston, she laughed and said, "We in Charleston are like the Chinese: We eat rice and we worship our ancestors." Her irreverence, only hinted at by her remarks, as well as her deep knowledge of Charleston, its people, its history, and all its foibles have kept us fast friends. Few have had more access to the ins and outs of the

city; after all, her family has lived in Charleston since the seventeenth century.

Kit, though, is no parochial Charlestonian. She's had a spectacular life that has taken her first from Charleston to Paris, where she slept on park benches and ended up cooking for the Black Panthers, to the Indian subcontinent where she's dined with maharajahs, and walked large portions of the Silk Road, and beyond. She's run a jewelry store on Madison Avenue in New York City and gone to Burmese pearl auctions. Now, she and her partner, Mary Silsby, own Lotus Flower, a floral design studio in the Holy City.

Kit is a formidable hostess, and her culinary repertoire reflects the breadth and depth of her travels. At her table, you might find a coq au vin one night and an Indonesian curry the next. To be fair, when one remembers Charleston has a history as a port and a connecting spot for many foodways, the curries and coq au vin are not that unexpected. Deeper Charleston traditions also make their way to the table. There might be venison, if a friend has brought some, or shad, the beloved but hard-to-fillet local fish. Her tastes are wide and ranging, but she is also a mistress of the traditional food of her youth; Kit avers that the food of Charleston came early to the American braid because of enslavement. She is very much aware of its connections to the folks that cooked it in the single and double houses owned by the city's elite. Kit recalls, "I lived in the kitchen at the house. I grew up in the kitchen." She continues, speaking of the formal British dining culture her family embodied:

> One of the amazing things about growing up in Charleston is that a lot of what we ate was considered to be from Africa. We didn't know it back then, but it was an important part of our heritage. My family had people who worked for us who were African American; they made dinner. I would come home from school around 2 in the afternoon, I would wash my hands and do all that, and then we would have dinner at 2:30. Dinner was a very formal affair. Later, we had supper, but supper was not formal at all. At dinner, there would be something like okra soup or fried oysters—we had Hoppin' John (field peas and rice) all the time. When I was a small child, we had vendors who would appear at back doors hawking food, like the shrimp man who came by with a tray. That was the way Charlestonians ate. There's not only British in the food of Charleston.

Unlike the British Puritans who settled in the northeastern sections of what would become the United States, who were of hardier stock and often worked the land themselves, the British folks who settled Charleston and the Lowcountry regions were more patrician and arrived with little knowledge of, or skill at, farming. Many of them, Kit's ancestors among them, had properties in both South Carolina and Barbados and toggled back and forth between them. Their vast land holdings were given over to the cultivation of rice, indigo, and long staple cotton, wealth-generating cash crops that were worked by the enslaved, and their kitchens were manned by them as well. The tastes of the African continent were also familiar to them because of their Caribbean sojourns, as is reflected in the African-derived recipes that are found in the early Colonial cookbooks from Carolina and Virginia. It was these tastes of the African continent that gave much of the cooking of Charleston and other parts of the Colonial South its unique flavor and created such touchstone Charleston dishes as okra soup, red rice, and Hoppin' John. In that sense, Kit's recipes, which follow, are highly indicative of the sort of British food of the era—deeply marked by their colonial exploits throughout the world at the time of their settling in this land.

Charleston was also a major port with a view to the world. "Charlestonians were traveling the world and they wanted to show people that they were sophisticated." So they created dishes that used curry and other exotic ingredients that arrived in their port from the Caribbean and beyond. Pineapples became symbols of hospitality; they were nailed on to front doors to signal a captain's return from a voyage and appeared not only on tables, but also carved into furniture and wrought in iron on entry gates.

Rice was king for centuries. Not only did the people of Charleston grow rice, but they also ate it at virtually every meal. "The Bennetts ate rice; we had rice every day. Others may have had shrimp and grits, we had shrimp and rice." The availability of rice and the numbers of different ways in which it was prepared resulted in the creation of a rice kitchen that still obtains in Charleston, and includes a range of rice breads and a multiplicity of rice dishes. Food scholar Karen Hess documented them in her book, *The Carolina Rice Kitchen,* and equally and correctly attributed the number of rice dishes to the African hands in the kitchen, and the remembrance of dishes from the rice coast of Africa that extends from southern Senegal through Liberia, the area from which many of the enslaved of the Lowcountry were taken. In the meals that Kit cooks and in the food of the city of her birth, rice has primacy and the flavors of the world mix and mingle.

CHARLESTON OKRA SOUP

SERVES 8

Although the first documented American recipe for okra soup is found in Mary Randolph's 1824 cookbook, *The Virginia Housewife*, the soup clearly has earlier origins in the West Indies and certainly harks back to the African continent where the vegetable originates. That okra soups were and are common in Charleston, South Carolina, and Savannah, Georgia, as well as Virginia is another indicator of just how deeply entwined the African and European threads of the American braid were in the South. In Charleston, okra soup is as common as gumbo is in New Orleans.

Made with beef (bone and meat) for savoriness and tomatoes for their sweet tartness, this recipe lets the okra itself shine. The acid from the tomato somewhat attenuates the slipperiness of the okra, but this is a recipe for okra lovers.

3 tablespoons olive oil

1¾ pounds beef bones with meat (neck bone or short rib)

2 white onions, medium diced

4 cups vegetable, beef, or chicken broth

2 (28-ounce) cans whole peeled tomatoes, undrained

1 bay leaf

3 pounds fresh okra, trimmed, and cut into rounds ½ inch thick

Kosher salt and freshly ground black pepper

Crumbled crisp-cooked bacon, for serving

1. In a large pot, heat 2 tablespoons of the oil over medium-high heat until shimmering. Add the meaty bones and cook for about 15 minutes, turning, until browned on all sides. Transfer to a plate.

2. Add the remaining 1 tablespoon oil to the pot and heat until it shimmers. Add the onions and cook, stirring, until lightly browned, 5 to 7 minutes.

3. Add the broth, tomatoes and their juices, bay leaf, and the meaty bones plus any accumulated juices. Reduce the heat to low and simmer until the tomatoes are broken down, about 1½ hours.

4. Stir in the okra and cook for 30 minutes more. Season well with salt and pepper. Discard the bay leaf. Remove the beef bones, using a fork to shred the meat and return that to the soup.

5. Serve hot, passing the bacon at the table.

OYSTER STEW

SERVES 4 TO 6

Oyster stew is often served on Christmas Eve in parts of the South. Made with milk and cream, it is the Southern cousin of some of the chowders served in New England; this one is thickened with a bit of roux and flavored subtly with celery and sherry, letting the dairy and briny taste of oysters shine.

The word chowder has a French etymology ("chowder" is an anglicization of *chaudron*, a French term for the cauldron in which the chowder was traditionally cooked). However, food historians believe that the dish had a binational origin with both Brittany in France and the Cornwall section of England, which faces it across the English Channel, being cited as its birthplace. The recipes for the thickened soupy stew were brought to the New World by mariners from both regions and caught on. Typically, chowders differ from soups in that they are thickened with milk or cream and flour. Defined as such, in the North, this recipe would be considered a chowder, but in Charleston, it's an oyster stew.

3 tablespoons salted butter

¾ cup diced celery

2 tablespoons all-purpose flour

4 cups whole milk

1 pint shucked oysters, with their liquor

2 small shallots, thinly sliced

Kosher salt

½ teaspoon freshly cracked black pepper

1 teaspoon cayenne pepper

¼ cup dry sherry

Chopped fresh parsley, for garnish

1. In a large saucepan, melt the butter over medium heat. Add the celery and cook until tender, a few minutes. Stir in the flour and cook until the celery looks matte. While whisking constantly, pour in a bit of the milk, stirring to form a smooth paste. Add the remaining milk, increase the heat to medium-high, and bring just to a boil.

2. Add the oysters, their liquor, and the shallots. Reduce the heat to medium-low and simmer for just a few minutes, until the oysters are heated through but not overcooked and mealy. Remove from the heat and season with salt to taste, the black pepper, and cayenne. Taste and adjust the seasoning to your preference.

3. Stir in the sherry and garnish with the parsley. Serve immediately, preferably in a hot bowl or mug.

SAUSAGE BISCUIT PINWHEELS

SERVES 4

This recipe is so ridiculously simple that it can be done by even the most ham-fisted of cooks. However, the results are delicious and like all perfect culinary shortcuts, if you don't tell, no one will know. Premade biscuit dough is rolled with a sausage filling, and then baked into an attractive pinwheel. These sausage biscuits might turn up atop an antique board for a hunt breakfast, alongside the more traditional ham biscuits that are also classic Southern fare.

And these sausage biscuits might also make an appearance at one of the myriad cocktail parties that rhythm the social year of the Holy City. Kit jokingly says that Charlestonians can eat a four-course meal off of a cocktail napkin.

1 (16.3-ounce) tube refrigerated biscuit dough, separated into 8 portions (see Note)

1 pound bulk sausage (hot, medium, or mild), crumbled, cooked, and well drained

1. Preheat the oven to 375°F. Grease a baking sheet with cooking spray or line it with parchment paper.

2. With a long side of the baking sheet facing you, arrange the biscuits in a two rows of 4 biscuits each, slightly overlapping, near the edge of the baking sheet closest to you, leaving at least 4 inches of open space on the pan. Gently press them together to make one large, solid rectangle. Make sure the edges of the biscuits are pressed together but not too much. (If you make the biscuit dough too thin, it will crack and leak as it bakes.)

3. Add the cooked sausage to the middle of the dough, leaving a ½-inch border. Roll the long edge of the biscuit dough toward the open space (away from you) to form a roll, creating a pinwheel effect inside. The roll should end up about in the center of the baking sheet.

4. Bake until nicely browned, 19 to 21 minutes.

5. Let the roll cool for 3 to 4 minutes before cutting into 8 equal slices. Serve warm.

NOTE: If using a tube of extra-large biscuits, reduce the oven temperature to 325°F and bake for 22 to 25 minutes. If using a larger 12-biscuit tube, such as a 24-ounce tube, simply use 8 biscuits for this recipe.

GARLIC

Garlic, *Allium sativum*, the pungent big daddy of the onion family, has been a culinary ingredient for millennia. In ancient Egypt, it was fed to the builders of the pyramids; it was given as offerings by the ancient Greeks and has been used in traditional medicine everywhere from China to Egypt. The sharpness of the bulb (also known as the stinking weed), though, has made it a no-fly zone for some cultures, and its use is rare in traditional English cuisine and the American cuisines that have developed from British threads. (The flavor of lamb, though, has a notable affinity for garlic, and so it's not uncommon to see slivers of it inserted into the meat of a roast.)

Garlic is of course a common ingredient in Mediterranean Europe, and has developed into a polarizing ingredient between foods of northern and southern Europe both on the continent and in this country. In our culture today, with its love of bold flavor, it's hard to imagine that garlic was avoided. But stories abound of, for instance, the American-born children of Italian immigrants in the early twentieth century trying to hide the stink of garlic from their clothes and breath.

Although Native peoples ate wild garlic prior to European contact, garlic as we know it is not native to this hemisphere and was brought by the Spanish, and featured in foods derived from that thread of the culinary braid. Likewise, it was used (albeit with subtlety) in French cooking. American culinary historian Waverley Root opines in his work *Eating in America* that as recently as the late 1920s, though, garlic in Anglo-inflected America was considered only for "ditch diggers." The reeking lily (for the plant is a member of the lily family) only begins to have more widespread culinary currency after 1940. Now, the culinary use of garlic in quantities large and small is considered a hallmark of gastronomic sophistication.

LAMB ROAST

SERVES 4 TO 6

Leg of lamb or a lamb roast is a celebration dish by anyone's standards. This version, which marinates the lamb in garlic, parsley, lime juice, and anchovies (these salty fish are many chefs' secret ingredient!), is then roasted with stock until tender and served with a rich jus. While Kit is fond of saying that "there's not much British in the food of Charleston," one can easily imagine this as an elegant Sunday roast on the tables of English families both today and centuries ago. The result is worthy of a mahogany dining table with elegant china, fine damask, and heavy silver. In Charleston style, it pairs perfectly with Red Rice (page 112).

1 (2-ounce) tin oil-packed anchovy fillets, drained

¼ cup fresh flat-leaf parsley, coarsely chopped

4 garlic cloves, crushed

Juice of 1 lime

¼ cup olive oil

4-pounds leg of lamb or lamb roasts

Kosher salt

1 teaspoon freshly ground black pepper

8 tablespoons (1 stick) salted butter

4 cups beef stock

1. In a food processor, combine the anchovies, parsley, garlic, lime juice, and oil and pulse 5 times to form a paste.

2. Use paper towels to pat the lamb dry. Season the meat with 1 tablespoon of salt and the pepper and rub with the anchovy paste. Place the lamb in a 1-gallon ziplock bag, seal, and massage to coat evenly. Marinate in the refrigerator for at least 2½ hours or up to 24 hours.

3. Preheat the oven to 425°F.

4. In a Dutch oven, melt the butter over medium-high heat. Remove the lamb from its bag and add it to the pot along with the marinade. Sear for a few minutes on all sides until evenly browned. Pour the stock around the meat and leave it over the heat until it comes to a simmer. Transfer to the oven.

5. Reduce the oven temperature to 350°F and roast, basting frequently, until the internal temperature registers 140°F on an instant-read thermometer, about 1½ hours. (If using lamb roasts, check after 30 minutes.)

6. Transfer the lamb to a cutting board and tent it with aluminum foil. Let the meat rest for about 30 minutes.

7. Pour the pan jus into a serving vessel and season to taste with salt. Thinly slice the meat and arrange it on a warmed platter. Pass the jus at the table.

RED RICE

SERVES 4 TO 6

Not only was rice South Carolina's primary cash crop for centuries, it also appeared on tables across the state almost three times a day. While rice is not traditionally a major part of the English table, in Charleston it takes primacy of place and a virtually untold number of rice dishes ranging from rice soups through purloos (or rice and pea dishes) to rice breads are a part of the city's culinary heritage.

Charleston's famous red rice is a connector between the cuisine of that city and that of Western Africa. Whether from Senegal or from Nigeria or Ghana, the taste for a rice dish made red with tomatoes and filled with vegetables crossed the ocean with enslaved Africans. As tomatoes are New World ingredients, it is thought the original reddening ingredient may have been red palm oil. But, by the time of the Transatlantic Slave Trade, tomatoes were in fair use on the African continent, and their use returned to the northern parts of the hemisphere in the recipes of the enslaved from the continent and the Caribbean.

South Carolina's vast wealth was based on its rice. Slave traders valued the technological and agricultural know-how of Africans from the rice-growing regions and enslaved them for work in Carolina's rice fields. The traditional African rice dishes were transformed into red rice and other bedrock staples of Gullah/Geechee cooking. Through the hands of the enslaved cooks, dishes like okra soup and red rice made their way onto the tables of the big house kitchens and thence into the culinary repertoire of all of the city's inhabitants.

Kit's preparation is simple but very delicious, started by cooking onions in rendered bacon fat, then cooking the rice in tomato-infused broth.

8 slices bacon

2 medium white onions, cut into ¼-inch dice

6 ounces (6 to 7 tablespoons) canned tomato paste

2 teaspoons sugar

2 teaspoons kosher salt

1 teaspoon crushed black pepper

2 cups long-grain white rice

4 cups water, low-sodium chicken broth, or low-sodium vegetable broth

1. Line a plate with paper towels. In a small Dutch oven, cook the bacon (in batches as needed) over medium heat until crisped. Transfer the bacon to the paper towels, keeping the rendered fat in the pot (about 8 tablespoons). Reserve the cooked bacon as a garnish or for another use.

2. Add the onions to the bacon fat and cook over medium heat until translucent, 3 to 4 minutes. Stir in the tomato paste and cook, stirring, for another 4 minutes to lightly caramelize.

3. Stir in the sugar, salt, and black pepper, continuing to stir until the sugar and salt have dissolved. Stir in the rice until it is well coated. Add the water and bring to a boil over medium-high heat. Reduce the heat to low, cover, and cook until the rice is tender and liquid is absorbed, 20 to 25 minutes.

4. Turn off the heat and allow to rest for 5 minutes, then fluff with a fork. Serve hot with the reserved bacon as a garnish.

OKRA

Wherever okra points its green tip, Africa has been, and the trail of trade evidenced by the presence of the pod is formidable. Our American use of the word okra comes from the Igbo language of Nigeria, where the plant is referred to as *okuru*. In France, the word for "okra" harks back to the Bantu languages, in which it is *ochingombo* and *kingombo*, but the French simply use the final two syllables, calling the mucilaginous pod *gombo*. It is a word that certainly resonates in southern Louisiana, where gumbos, many of which contain okra, are rife and as varied as the cultures that met and melded there.

Okra probably was first introduced into the continental United States via Louisiana, and R. W. Schery in *Plants for Man* postulated that okra was brought to the New World by the French in the 1700s. Others suggest the Portuguese brought it to this hemisphere and place its introduction in the sixteenth century. Whoever is responsible for the pod's presence in this hemisphere, by 1748 it was being used in Philadelphia; in 1781 Thomas Jefferson commented on it as growing in Virginia, and we now know that it was certainly grown in the slave gardens of Monticello. (It also appeared on the master's table if we are to trust *The Virginia Housewife* by Mary Randolph, who includes a recipe for Gumbs: A West India Dish.) By 1806, the plant is in relatively widespread use, and botanists are speaking of several different varieties of it.

Okra is relatively high in nutritional value and rich in calcium, phosphorus, potassium, and iron. Okra is easy to digest, mildly laxative, and has emollient properties. Dried okra can be found as far afield as the bazaars of the Middle East and the homes of the Gullah/Geechee of the Carolina/Georgia Lowcountry, where the pods are dried and strung garland-like along with shrimp heads to provide seasoning and thickening for their roux-less gumbos.

Still, okra suffers from a lack of respect in the contemporary American culinary world—it is the Rodney Dangerfield of vegetables!—due to its propensity toward ooze. Like the Africans and their descendants who came to revere it in almost totemic capacity, okra does not behave. It is tricky. It cannot be tamed into submission by the cook who does not know how to use it properly. The sticky substance that some abhor is exuded out with every cut. The more okra is cut, the more it's sticky. The prodigious thickening properties of this gel mean that okra can take a thin watery soup and transform it into a substantial one. Those who are hell-bent on defying okra's natural propensity toward ooze can fry it, as they do in much of the South, or blanch young tender pods and serve them in a salad with a light vinaigrette, as they do in parts of Brazil. It is said that a squeeze of lemon juice or of a bit of vinegar in the cooking water will cut down the stick, but let's stop fighting the mucilaginous vegetable and let okra do its own magnificent thing.

APPLES

There are literally thousands of varieties of the common apple, *Malus domestica.* The fruit, thought to have originated in Kazakhstan, is botanically complex, so the only way to ensure that a plant is like its parent plants is by grafting.

No one is sure how crab apples arrived in our land, but there are actually three species of crab apple that are native to North America. Apples as we know them made their way to these lands in the 1600s, with the Pilgrims who settled in what would become Massachusetts. They brought young apple trees from England and planted seedling orchards; Lord Baltimore in the Maryland colony advised settlers to bring with them seeds of pears and apples for making cider and perry. By 1644, 90 percent of Maryland farms had apple orchards. The first orchard in Massachusetts had been planted just eleven years earlier. The seeds distributed by the real-life Johnny Appleseed, John Chapman of Leominster, Massachusetts, created orchards that produced a wide-ranging selection of apples in areas of the Midwest.

In the early years, apples were not just snacked on, but found their ways into all manner of cooking: They were fried, baked, stewed, made into preserves, apple butters, and apple sauces. They were dried in the sun and stowed for long winters and, of course, they appeared in the iconically American apple pie. Their juice was transformed into vinegars, brandies, and most vitally, ciders, which were consumed like water.

In the nineteenth century, the fruit varied widely in size and shape, and there were over fourteen thousand varieties. Slowly, however, the Red Delicious and Golden Delicious and Granny Smith apples that were commercially produced became, functionally speaking, the only mainstream apples. However, a resurgence of heirloom varieties like the Roxbury Russet—and the emergence of newer, developed-for-market varieties like Honeycrisp—may mean that there will be a more diverse crop of apples in the future.

HUGUENOT TORTE

SERVES 16

Huguenot torte is probably Charleston's most famous dessert. It is however neither Huguenot nor a torte, but rather something a bit like the love child of apple crisp and pecan pie. A light batter barely holds a combination of equal parts apples and pecans, baked until crisp and browned on top, almost meringue-like. A dollop of whipped cream finishes the sweet-tart dessert.

The dish seems to be derived from something known as Ozark pudding, which was a favorite dessert of Harry Truman. The recipe first appears under the name Huguenot Torte in 1950 in *Charleston Receipts*, the city's legendary community cookbook. It became the signature dish for the Huguenot Tavern, a Charleston restaurant where the recipe's originator, Evelyn Anderson Florance, worked. The tavern became known for the dessert, which was named to honor the Huguenots—Protestant French who were among the first settlers in Charleston. Its recipe has been shared far and wide.

Softened butter, for greasing

4 large eggs, at room temperature

3 cups sugar

½ cup all-purpose flour

5 teaspoons baking powder

½ teaspoon kosher salt

2 cups chopped tart peeled apples

2 cups chopped pecans, plus more for garnish

2 teaspoons vanilla extract

Whipped cream, for serving

1. Preheat the oven to 325°F. Generously butter two 8 × 12-inch baking pans.

2. In a stand mixer fitted with the whisk, beat the eggs and sugar on medium speed, just until frothy. Switch to the paddle and on low speed, gradually beat in the flour until combined. Add the baking powder, salt, apples, pecans, and vanilla, beating just until incorporated and the batter is slightly thick.

3. Divide the batter evenly between the two prepared pans.

4. Bake until browned and crusty and the tortes are just set, 20 to 25 minutes.

5. Let the cakes cool in the pans for 30 minutes, then turn them out onto a cooling rack to cool for another 30 minutes.

6. Serve topped with whipped cream and a sprinkling of chopped pecans.

THE FOOD HISTORIAN

PETER ROSE

Peter G. Rose is an outlier in my listing of people who make up the American braid in that she is not a descendant of the Dutch in the United States, but rather Dutch by birth. She, though, got a pass from me because she is the leading specialist in the food of the Dutch experience in America. (She has also lived in the United States for fifty years.) She was kind enough to speak to me after being recommended by my friend, the late forensic archeologist and general food maven, Daphne Derven, who for many decades was one of my culinary secret weapons. Another of them, the late Nach Waxman, of Kitchen Arts and Letters, the legendary New York culinary bookstore, said of her, "Peter Rose knows more about Dutch life and lore than anyone I've ever come across . . ."

The Dutch are the foundational members of the American braid that we often forget, because the Dutch hide in plain sight. It's not that there are no descendants of those who arrived on these shores from the Low Countries, it's just that they are less often thought of or mentioned in histories as having had an important role in the founding of what would become the United States.

Those who live in New York, however, are reminded daily of their presence by the preponderance of Dutch names across the city: Lefferts Boulevard, the Van Wyck Expressway, Bedford-Stuyvesant, Van Rensselaer and Phillipsburg Manors, the Knickerbocker Club, Harlem, and more. Even the New York Yankees owe their name to the Dutch. (One explanation is that Jan, meaning John, was a common Dutch name, so much so that it became a kind of Dutchmen. Jan is pronounced "Yan," and "Janke" is a diminutive, meaning "little John.") The Dutch and their cultural spore are most visible north of New York City, in Washington Irving country, where you can almost hear the laughter of the headless horseman as he chases Ichabod Crane and sense the bonhomie of the good burghers of New Netherland at every turn. You can feel their presence in Albany and in areas upstate where Pinkster, an African American take on the Dutch holiday of Pentecost (Pinksteren), is still celebrated in late May or early June. Even so, most of us would be hard pressed to recall that Henry Hudson's explorations enabled the Dutch to claim an area known as New Netherland that once stretched from the Connecticut River to Delaware Bay.

This, then, is the bailiwick of Peter Rose; she has studied many of the twelve thousand documents that remain from this period and form the basis of what is now known as the New Netherland Research Center in Albany. In fact, it is from Rose and her exacting translations of many of these documents that we know much about the food and foodways of the early Dutch settlers.

Rose began as a food historian, as I did, in the days when there were no degrees in Food Studies or in Gastronomy. She explains:

> When I started as a food historian, nobody was trained in it. We had to kind of find our way and make discoveries in many ways. We used logic and figured it out. It may not be this, but maybe it's that. Sometimes, we just made an educated guess and then many years later found out that our educated guess was absolutely spot on. That's how it used to be.

The world of food historians and food history has changed immensely.

Rose, as one of the founding mothers of the discipline in the United States, set some of the standards. She had to learn how to cook on an open hearth to be able to translate the old recipes into ones that could be used by modern cooks in modern kitchens. She has always been meticulous in her research, sometimes relying on instinct to fill in where there simply were no paths or leads. Sometimes something as simple as reading a word aloud might create a connection that had not occurred when reading it silently on the written page. All of this, not to mention her mastery of old Dutch, created a formidable arsenal of research tools that have resulted in her nine books that detail the foodways of the early Dutch and their foundational role in some of the cooking of the United States.

It was from Peter that I learned that the coleslaw that accompanies the hamburgers at many a July Fourth cookout is really a derivation of the Dutch *koolsla,* meaning "cabbage salad," as attested to by an eighteenth-century recipe. From her, I gleaned that America's Santa Claus, as opposed to the British Father Christmas, is a close cousin of the Sinterklaas of the Netherlands, and that the cookies that are shared during the holiday season are really descendants of the *koekje* or *koekie* meaning "little cake." And then, the waffles that go under the chicken and waffles that has become an African American—now American—classic are also owed to the folks from the Low Countries.

We owe many unspoken culinary connections to the Dutch, and to their vast trading empire that made New Netherland a trade hub and created a cosmopolitan life in downtown New York City that was unequaled. We also owe a debt to Peter Rose and others like her who have so carefully catalogued their contributions.

COLESLAW
WITH BUTTER VINAIGRETTE

SERVES 4 TO 6

In her book, *History on Our Plate: Recipes from America's Dutch Past for Today's Cook*, culinary historian Peter Rose reports that, "When Swedish botanist Pehr (Peter) Kalm visited the Dutch in the Albany area in the mid-eighteenth century, he described in his diary being served a dish by his landlady that was unknown to him. It consisted of the finely cut inner leaves of cabbage, mixed with a warm dressing. He adds that for this dish 'butter is frequently used.' The butter was mixed with vinegar and kept warm in a pot by the fire. This was our present-day coleslaw; the word 'coleslaw' comes from the Dutch *kool* (Dutch for 'cabbage') and *sla* (Dutch for 'slaw' or 'salad')." Serve it as a side dish or of course, with fish and French fries.

I am fascinated by this recipe, as it is very close to the coleslaw I grew up with, which had none of the raisins or carrots or other additions that many current variants contain, just cabbage and dressing. I now wonder where my mother got her recipe. Of course, the unusual butter vinaigrette here gives this slaw a richness of flavor; try to make sure the cabbage is not ice-cold from the refrigerator when you dress it, as that would harden the butter and make for a less pleasant mouthfeel.

¼ head green cabbage, at room temperature, cut into thin strips or shredded (2 cups)

¼ head red cabbage, at room temperature, cut into thin strips or shredded (2 cups)

4 tablespoons (½ stick) salted butter

½ cup white wine vinegar

¼ teaspoon sugar

Kosher salt and freshly ground black pepper

1. In a large bowl, toss together the green and red cabbages.

2. In a medium saucepan, melt the butter over medium heat. Stir in the vinegar and sugar, stirring until the sugar has dissolved. Season with salt and pepper to taste.

3. Pour the mixture over the cabbage and toss to coat evenly. Allow the coleslaw to stand for at least 1 hour before serving.

4. Taste for seasoning and add more salt if needed. Toss again before serving.

YEASTED BELGIAN WAFFLES

SERVES 4 TO 6

These waffles can, of course, be made in an electric waffle iron, but they are even more fun to make in the fireplace using an old-fashioned long-handled waffle iron, if you happen to own one. Just be sure to preheat the iron and to grease it with butter before each use, or the waffles will stick and you'll have a mess on your hands. These waffles are more bread-like than modern ones and not quite as light. In the seventeenth century they were served plain or with butter.

The 1964 World's Fair in New York City introduced Belgian waffles to the general public and popularized them once again. (Remember, Belgium was a part of the Low Countries.)

Today, one of the great examples of the modern American braid and a newer use of the Dutch waffle is in the African American specialty chicken and waffles. That dish is thought to have originated at Wells, a late-night spot in Harlem (the neighborhood itself was originally named after the Dutch city of Haarlem). The origin story goes that when African American jazz musicians returned from their gigs, they craved something that would be a bit of breakfast and a bit of dinner . . . fried chicken atop a waffle . . . voilà, a contemporary classic that embodies the American braid was born.

2¼ teaspoons (1 envelope) active dry yeast

¼ cup warm water (100° to 110°F)

Pinch of sugar

4 cups all-purpose flour

6 tablespoons (¾ stick) unsalted butter, melted and cooled

2 cups whole milk

2 large eggs, lightly beaten

Syrup of your choice and melted butter, for serving

1. In a small bowl, sprinkle the yeast over the warm water and add the sugar. Let stand for 2 minutes, then stir to dissolve the sugar. Transfer to a warm place to rest for 5 minutes, until bubbly. If the mixture doesn't get foamy, try again with new yeast.

2. Place the flour in a large bowl, make a well in the center, and add the yeast mixture and 4 tablespoons of the melted butter, stirring to combine. Gradually stir in the milk and the eggs to form a batter. Let sit for 30 minutes or up to 1 hour.

3. Preheat a waffle iron. Using the remaining 2 tablespoons melted butter, brush the hot iron to grease it. Pour batter into the iron (consult your waffle iron's instructions for the correct quantity). Close the lid and cook until golden; the timing depends on the type and size of the waffle iron—again, consult the iron's instructions.

4. Serve warm with syrup and more melted butter if you'd like.

KANDEEL

MAKES ABOUT 1 QUART

The early settlers in Dutch America were not averse to an occasional tipple (remember Rip Van Winkle?), and what more perfect time than the birth of a baby to raise a glass in a toast? This traditional celebratory drink for the time a baby is born is still very much a part of Dutch culinary tradition. Kandeel was still served by the royal family when the Crown Prince (now King) Willem-Alexander of the Netherlands was born in 1967.

With its strong use of sweet spices—a luxury at the time of its creation—and a rich base of thickened egg yolks, this is like a mulled wine married to eggnog.

Recipes for this festive drink appear under the anglicized name "condale" in several of the scrap/cookbooks that were handed down in families of the descendants of the first Dutch settlers of Nieuw Nederland, reflecting their assimilation of some English ways.

10 whole cloves

¼ teaspoon ground mace

¼ teaspoon freshly grated nutmeg

2 (3-inch) cinnamon sticks, plus more for serving

Strips of zest from 1 lemon, removed with a vegetable peeler

6 large egg yolks, at room temperature

½ cup sugar

1 (750 ml) bottle medium-dry white Rhine wine (about 3 cups)

1. In a small saucepan, combine 1½ cups water, the cloves, mace, nutmeg, cinnamon sticks, and lemon zest. Cover and simmer over low heat for 1 hour. Strain through a fine-mesh sieve set over a bowl (discard the solids).

2. In a deep saucepan, heat a few inches of water over medium heat, until just simmering. Set a heatproof bowl on top that does not touch the water below. Add the egg yolks and sugar and whisk for several minutes, until foamy and the sugar has dissolved.

3. Whisk in the strained spice liquid, until the mixture thickens. Gradually whisk in the wine.

4. Ladle into glasses or mugs. Serve hot. If the drink separates upon standing, stir with a spoon or a tall cinnamon stick.

TEA COOKIES

MAKES 120 SMALL COOKIES

Cookies in all sizes, shapes, and flavors are everywhere, from the industrial ones that line the shelves of grocery stores and supermarkets to the ones prepared from exotic ingredients that come from small artisanal bakeries. We trade them at Christmas, give them out at birthdays, and consume tons of those sold annually by the Girl Scouts. Who would guess that the name of this seemingly American confection—and indeed the treat itself—would originate with the Dutch? *Koekje* means "little cake," and when you say the word aloud, the English "cookie" comes to the ear.

This recipe offered by Rose originates from Maria Sanders van Rensselaer (1749–1830), who spelled them as, in half-English, half-Dutch fashion: "cookjes." The original recipe from her handwritten book reads: "½ butt ¾ sugar 1 teacup water as much flour as it takes." With such simple ingredients, you might not imagine that these cookies would be any good, but they are!

16 tablespoons (2 sticks) lightly salted butter, at room temperature

1½ cups sugar

¾ cup cold water

3½ cups all-purpose flour

1. In a stand mixer fitted with the paddle, beat the butter on medium speed for several minutes, until fluffy and lightened. Gradually add the sugar, beating until combined. Stop to scrape down the bowl.

2. On low speed, alternate adding the water and the flour, beating to form a slightly sticky dough. Wrap the dough and refrigerate for 1 hour.

3. Preheat the oven to 350°F. Line several baking sheets with parchment paper.

4. Unwrap the dough and divide it in half, keeping the remaining dough chilled. Portion the dough half into 60 portions, each big enough to make a ½-inch ball. Roll them into balls and place them ½ inch apart on the baking sheets.

5. Bake one sheet at a time until lightly browned at the edges, 8 to 10 minutes.

6. Cool on the sheet for 5 minutes and transfer to a wire rack. Repeat to use all the dough, letting the baking sheets cool before using again. Let cool slightly and serve warm. Store leftover cookies in an airtight container at room temperature.

DOUGHNUTS
OLYKOEKS

MAKES 25 TO 30 SMALL DOUGHNUTS

We know these Dutch confections better as doughnuts, but they are still known as *olykoeks* ("oil cakes") even today in some parts of the Hudson Valley in New York State. They are very similar to old-fashioned plain doughnuts. Here, they are finished with a coating of sugar. Again, as with waffles and cookies, the surprise is that these oil cakes that are the ancestors of our doughnut are a culinary gift from the Dutch. Imagine, if you will, a national chain of shops named Dunkin' Olykoeks.

3 envelopes active dry yeast (2 tablespoons plus ¾ teaspoon)

¼ cup warm water (100° to 110°F)

¾ cup sugar, plus more for coating

8 tablespoons (1 stick) salted butter, at room temperature

3 large eggs, at room temperature

1 cup whole milk

4 cups all-purpose flour

3 quarts vegetable oil, for frying

1. In a small bowl, sprinkle the yeast over the warm water and add a pinch of the sugar. Let stand for 2 minutes, then stir to dissolve the sugar. Transfer to a warm place to rest for 5 minutes, until bubbly. If the mixture does not get foamy, try again with new yeast.

2. In a stand mixer fitted with the paddle, beat the butter and ¾ cup sugar on medium speed until fluffy and lightened. Stop to scrape down the bowl. Add the eggs one at a time, beating until combined. Add the milk and the yeast mixture. Gradually stir in the flour (or mix in on low speed), beating to form a dough.

3. Cover and let rise in a warm spot until doubled in bulk, about 1 hour.

4. Pour 4 inches of oil into a large deep pot and heat to 350°F (or use a deep-fryer). Line a baking sheet with paper towels and add a wire rack. Fill a medium bowl halfway with sugar for coating.

5. Working in batches of 4 or 5 olykoeks at a time, dip a soup spoon into the hot oil and use it to scoop a heaping spoonful of dough (repeat this action for every scoop; this way the dough will not stick). Holding the spoon just above the hot oil, carefully push off the dough with the aid of another spoon and fry, turning them over once, until golden brown, 3 to 4 minutes. Check one olykoek by cutting it in half to see if it is cooked through.

6. Transfer to the paper towels to drain. Roll each olykoek in the bowl of sugar to coat.

7. Serve as a snack or for breakfast.

FIRSTBORN SON

LOUIS COSTA

Not everyone can claim to own a tomato-red velvet tailcoat, but my friend Louis Costa has one hanging in his closet. He used to don it when he led the parade for the Creole Tomato Festival, which he inaugurated when he was the head of the French Market in New Orleans. Lou is, as you may guess, a true food lover and a character. His house in the Muses, as the area of Coliseum Square in the Lower Garden District is called, used to be a Freedmen's Bureau. Its high-ceiling double parlors have been featured in art and design books about the city, and are treasure troves of family heirlooms and glorious art. (Lou's wife, Mary Len, an artist herself, was for a time the head of the city's Arts Council.) Lou is the father of what I can already call a culinary dynasty, for he, his wife, daughter, and grandchildren all delight in the arts of the kitchen.

The family butcher-block counter is piled high with cookbooks, magazines, and the detritus from years of cooking: tin boxes for the cheese straws that Mary Len bakes and distributes to friends, the sheet pans for the king cakes that she also makes. The "guava lava" cake is a spectacular and particularly delicious mix of the American braid: The recipe fills a twist of French brioche dough with guava paste

and queso blanco. They are the dynamic duo of Louisiana food in my book, and my adopted family in that city.

I met the Costas too many years ago to count, but at least three decades have passed since I've begun watching their daughter, Lenora, grow from a poised eight-year-old, to now being a mother herself.

Once, when I asked about the ethnicity of Lou's ancestors, he simply replied, "European, North American, Colonial French, et cetera. I don't know. I mean, it's hard to say. Technically French, but they're actually half English—with a little sprinkling of German in there—and the other half is Italian." Lou's reaction is not unusual in a city where many people know their six times great-grandparents and carry their ancestry as a badge of honor in the streets. But when I pressed him about his family origins he finally revealed:

My fifth great-grandfather, Claude Jousset de la Loire, was born in 1704 in Mobile, Alabama. As an adult, he was recognized and given the stipend provided by the French government as the first French male child born in Louisiana. The rumor was that another boy was born earlier, but died as an infant. Of course, his wife's brother-in-law being chairman of the Superior Council had

*nothing to do with this resolution. He really
was the first surviving male child in the
colony. Claude's father was Jean-Baptiste,
who came to Louisiana with Bienville, and
his father was Mathurin who was one of the
early settlers of Montreal.*

So, amazingly, my friend Lou is a direct
descendant of the first surviving French male
child born in French Louisiana! Perhaps that's
where he gets his love of cooking.

That love is manifested in creative meals that
he makes all year round. Summer means lovely
tomato salads prepared with wonderfully fresh
Creole tomatoes, the ones for which he'd donned
the red tailcoat so many years ago. There's always
fig jam from the fig trees, fig preserves, and one
year, a fig liqueur prepared from the fig leaves.
Lemon curd can be had, and occasionally there
are small jars of goose fat, but I feel that much
of this is Mary Len's doing. Easter means oyster
patties, carefully created in flaky pastry shells,
and Thanksgiving means two different kinds of
stuffing: oyster and corn bread.

This all culminates in the pull-out-all-the-
stops Christmas dinners that Lou's done for
more than twenty years. The planning involves
spreadsheets, consulting multiple cookbooks,
and sourcing items from far-flung purveyors.
One year, cock's combs were required to prepare
a gelatin. Lou journeyed to a Vietnamese market
in New Orleans East and tried to find them by
waving his fingers on the top of his head and
crowing. Another year, I was saluted with a
dinner based solely on recipes from my books.
But the most memorable ones were the two that
were about Lou's own origin story, with dishes

from the Loire region of France and others from
French Canada.

And that origin story brings us to this: Lou is
an only child and someone who shares with me
what I refer to as the dreaded archival gene. He
is therefore the custodian of his family recipes.
They are a treasure trove of historic recipes
that go back several generations, representing
the food of Louisiana as it was prepared in
Creole households. Some have a preserved-in-
amber quality to them in their richness of taste,
selection of ingredients, and preferred cooking
methods. His family recipes come from that same
culinary ethos. Written down on index cards
and annotated by each successive generation,
they are the distillation of culinary memory. Lou
shared a selection of these for this book, which
showcase his family's love of celebration and
the traditional foods that come with it, as well
as their custodianship of some of New Orleans's
most beloved recipes.

While New Orleans food only represents a
portion of the influence that French cooking
has had on the food of the United States, the
longevity of the nation's culinary influence is
represented in the cooking pots of that city.
From those early in the nation's history who
displayed their sophistication by having French-
trained chefs like Thomas Jefferson's James
Hemings, to those who even today use French
terms real and imagined on menus and serve
dishes *au jus* and *en papillote,* the country of
la Varenne and Escoffier casts an enormous
shadow over the cooking of the United States.
Lou Costa, his family, and their recipes represent
an important piece of their story.

NEW ORLEANS VEAL DAUBE

SERVES 4 TO 6

The usual New Orleans variant of the beef braise daube is a conjoining of the French and Italian (specifically Sicilian) threads that run deep in the city's culinary history. Indeed, New Orleans food expert Dale Curry opines that the local daube is just a pot roast cooked in the spaghetti sauce that is known in town as "red gravy."

Of course, the French "daube" *sounds* more refined than "pot roast," whether that is true or not. The Costas's version is more akin to the classic French braise—tomato is nowhere to be found and only two of southern Louisiana's culinary trinity (green bell pepper and onion, no celery) are used. The quality of the meat is vital here, as this recipe is seasoned simply to let the flavor of the meat shine. Don't skimp on the searing; take your time to do so and make sure all sides are deeply browned, as that is key to developing a rich flavor. The thrifty Creoles had a second-day leftover version of the daube recipe, called a daube glacé, with the leftovers of the stew cooked down and chilled into a sliceable gelatin of herbs, vegetables, and meat.

2 tablespoons vegetable shortening

3-pound bone-in veal shank or 2-pound boneless veal shoulder roast

Kosher salt

1 cup chopped onion

1 green bell pepper, chopped

2 bay leaves

4 fresh parsley sprigs

Fresh thyme sprigs

Worcestershire sauce

½ cup dry sherry or Madeira

1 tablespoon salted butter, at room temperature

1. In a large Dutch oven, melt the shortening over medium-high heat. Season the meat all over with 2 teaspoons salt and add it to the pot, turning as needed to sear it on all sides until deeply browned, about 15 minutes total.

2. Add 6 cups water (or enough to just cover the meat) and the onion to the pot. Bring to a boil over high heat. Reduce the heat to a slow simmer, cover, and simmer for 1 hour.

3. Add the bell pepper, bay leaves, parsley, thyme, and a few dashes of Worcestershire sauce to the liquid in the pot. Cover and cook until fork-tender, about 1½ hours.

4. Transfer the meat to a cutting board and tent it with aluminum foil. Let it rest for about 15 minutes.

5. Meanwhile, continue simmering the liquid until it's reduced to a jus. Add the sherry and salt to taste and simmer for 10 minutes.

6. Set a fine-mesh sieve over a bowl to strain the jus, discarding any solids. Finish the jus by whisking in the butter.

7. Slice the meat against the grain and serve with the jus.

STEWED TURNIPS, POTATOES, AND PORK

SERVES 2 TO 4

As a fan of all things turnip and a card-carrying lover of swine in all forms, I was delighted when Lou told me of his grandmother's dish of diced turnips and potatoes that she traditionally served with pork chops. Here, they are all cooked together in a delicious stew that combines the sweet/tangy taste of the turnips with the smoothness of potato and the savoriness of the pork. It is similar to some of the stews from the Normandy region, but uses water instead of the Norman cider. An economical dish, this is in the tradition of vegetable dishes that use meat as a seasoning rather than as the main component.

2 boneless pork shoulder chops, cut into ½-inch cubes

Kosher salt and freshly ground black pepper

1 tablespoon vegetable or olive oil

1 small onion, cut into ¼-inch dice

2½ pounds turnips, peeled and cut into ½-inch pieces

1 pound Yukon Gold potatoes, scrubbed well and cut into ½-inch pieces

1 garlic clove, minced

3 fresh thyme sprigs

1 bay leaf

1. Season the chops on both sides with salt and pepper.

2. In a deep sauté pan, heat the oil over medium-high heat until shimmering. Add the pork and spread out in one layer. Sear until golden brown, about 3 minutes.

3. Add the onion and cook, stirring occasionally, until translucent, about 3 minutes. Add the turnips, potatoes, garlic, thyme, bay leaf, and ½ teaspoon pepper. Cook, stirring occasionally, until the vegetables are nicely browned, 10 to 15 minutes.

4. Reduce the heat to medium, add 2 cups water, cover, and simmer until the potatoes and turnips are tender, 15 to 20 minutes. Discard the thyme and bay leaf. The sauce should be reduced to almost half.

5. Season with salt and pepper to taste and serve.

POUPONNE D'ANTILLY'S CALAS

MAKES 3 DOZEN CALAS

Calas and beignets (see page 140) are New Orleans's two classic fritters. While most people know the more traditional French beignet, which has garnered fame at the Café du Monde and become a must-have food for many visitors to the Crescent City, the cala—a rice fritter that probably has African origins—is less well known. What *is* known is that calas are delicious: Crisp but soft, the fritters are mild and lovely with a dusting of powdered sugar. And it is *also* known that, in the complicated world of Colonial New Orleans, some of the enslaved possessed the right to buy their own freedom. And because of this, and the fact that they were customarily given Sundays as a day of rest, enslaved women could be seen selling fresh, hot calas in front of the cathedral, saving their earnings to use to purchase their freedom and that of members of their families. Freewomen would sell them as well.

A treasured early recipe from the Costa collection is the one that Lou gave me for calas. It is a recipe from Pouponne d'Antilly, a cook in Lou's ancestor's Julie Bertin d'Antilly's household. The Costas do not know if Pouponne was a free person of color or enslaved, but her calas have come down in the Costa family as a treasured family recipe that are still made today.

2 quarts vegetable oil, for frying

2 cups cooked rice, cooled

3 large eggs, lightly beaten, at room temperature

1½ cups self-rising flour

½ cup granulated sugar

½ teaspoon kosher salt

Freshly grated nutmeg

½ cup warm milk (100° to 110°F)

1 teaspoon vanilla extract

Powdered sugar, for serving

1. Set a wire rack over a sheet pan or line a sheet pan with paper towels. In a Dutch oven, heat the oil over medium-high heat to 350°F.

2. In a bowl, stir together the rice, eggs, flour, granulated sugar, salt, and the nutmeg to taste until well combined. Stir in the warm milk and vanilla to form a smooth batter.

3. Working in batches to not crowd the pot, drop tablespoons of the batter, one at a time, into the hot oil. Cook for 3 minutes on the first side, turn them over, and cook for 2 minutes on the second side, until golden brown.

4. Transfer to the wire rack or paper towels to drain briefly. Dust with the powdered sugar and serve immediately.

SUGAR

Humans have long evidenced a longing for the sweet. There is a theory that suggests the desire for sweetness is hardwired in our brains; sweetness signifying sugar and the availability of easy calories—a boon to survival. This taste has been satisfied by sweeteners ranging from the maple syrup used by Native peoples in the northeastern United States and bees' honey used around the world. None, though, have attained the international primacy of sugar. It arrived in this hemisphere and in what would become the United States with the Spanish.

Sugar from cane is so much part of our lives that we take it for granted. We consume a staggering sixty-six to eighty-eight pounds of it per person annually, in a variety of guises. In the United States, we are considered slackers when compared to the figures for places like Australia, Cuba, and Brazil.

Sugarcane has been known for at least 2,200 years, and is an adaptable plant that can grow upwards of fifteen feet tall. It is tolerant of a wide variety of soil conditions and can grow on both hillsides and flat lands.

The story of how sugarcane moved around the world is riveting and well told in the books *Bittersweet: The Story of Sugar* by historian Peter Macinnis and *Sweetness and Power: The Place of Sugar in Modern History* by anthropologist Sidney Mintz. It was first brought to the western hemisphere by Columbus in 1493 and his diaries remark on the abundant harvest, but it seems that he had no interest in cultivating it on a large scale. That wouldn't happen in the Caribbean until the seventeenth century, and that brought the plantation system, enslavement, and all of its horrors to the hemisphere.

While the Triangle Trade of sugar, rum (made from sugar), and enslaved people (purchased with the rum) fundamentally wrote the story of the beginning of our nation, cane as a profitable crop only entered the United States in the early nineteenth century, and became very much a part of life in southern Louisiana. Brought by the Jesuits in the mid-1700s, it was not successful as a venture and only gained footing later in the century when Étienne de Boré introduced sugar-refining to Louisiana, Norbert Rillieux developed an evaporation-pan process, and other technological advances allowed sugar production to flourish in Louisiana.

But profit also brought what Macinnis calls the four curses of sugar: 1) It is capital intensive; 2) speed is necessary when processing the crop; 3) it is hungry for fuel; and 4) it is labor-intensive. The result is an industry that did, and does, deplete natural resources, require extraordinary capital outlays, and that is generally unconcerned about human life. When cane is in harvest in southern Louisiana and Florida, the mills work twenty-four hours a day and the smell of cane and burning cane trash lingers in the air. It is a classic smell of the Gulf South, and a very American smell.

CARNIVAL BEIGNETS

MAKES 8 BEIGNETS

Beignet is a French word for "fritter"—any fritter. In New Orleans, the word has come to mean the puffed pillows of dough coated with powdered sugar that are a late-night or breakfast treat. If calas (see page 136) may have an African origin, beignets are undeniably French. This recipe, using a self-rising flour, is a quick version of the classic yeasted fritters that many think of when they think of New Orleans. The recipe come from Lou's great-grandmother Blanche Livaudais Tronchet (1863–1933), and the notation on the recipe says that the beignets were traditionally served at Carnival time, which is also known as Mardi Gras season. Whenever you have them, have them with coffee. Perhaps pair them with calas and savor the difference in taste between the airy beignets and the more substantial calas. Whichever you prefer, they are twin avatars of New Orleans culinary history.

1. Set a wire rack into a sheet pan and have nearby. In a Dutch oven or deep-fryer, heat the oil over medium heat to 350°F. Place the powdered sugar in a large bowl.

2. In a medium bowl, whisk together the eggs, melted butter, granulated sugar, and rum. Add the flour, salt, and milk, mixing to form a soft dough.

3. Working in batches to not crowd the pot, gently drop ¼ cup of the dough into the hot oil, one at a time. Cook until the beignets begin to rise to the top and become golden brown, 2 to 3 minutes. Turn them over and cook another 2 to 3 minutes, until fully puffed and golden.

4. Transfer to the wire rack to drain briefly, then drop them one at a time into the bowl of powdered sugar, turning to coat the beignets on each side.

5. Serve warm, dusted with more powdered sugar.

2 quarts vegetable oil, for frying

½ cup powdered sugar, for serving

2 large eggs, at room temperature

4 tablespoons (½ stick) unsalted butter, melted and slightly cooled

2 tablespoons granulated sugar

2 tablespoons dark rum

1½ cups self-rising flour

1 teaspoon kosher salt

1 tablespoon milk

COFFEE

Whether it's consumed in a fancy porcelain cup, in a Starbucks canister, or a blue and white paper vessel straight from the local deli, coffee is the liquid that fuels countless mornings in the United States. Many people, though, who are gulping down the sustaining beverage in an attempt to be awake enough to get to work, don't know that the beans that made their coffee are originally African.

The coffee bean originates in Ethiopia and a legend tells the story of frolicking goats (obviously enjoying their caffeine high), who led a goatherd named Kaldi to a bush with its miraculous red berries. After eating the berries, he too experienced increased energy. The word spread and later, monks came to use the berries to stay awake for longer devotions. As the berries' fame grew, they began to be transformed into a variety of foodstuffs; over the centuries they were mixed with animal fat, fermented into a form of wine, and eventually their seeds were roasted to create the beverage that we know today. Many, though, as they savor that second cup of what is sometimes called the wine of Islam, forget that it is one of Africa's gifts to the culinary world.

NEW ORLEANS RUM BABAS

SERVES 4

Julie Tronchet Masson, Lou's grandmother, and Myldred Masson Costa, his mother, were family matriarchs who seemingly had a sweet tooth. The rum babas would have been served at the end of a meal or as a special treat. Myldred Masson Costa would pour a little more rum on top of them just prior to serving

The classic French *baba au rhum* was created by a chef for Stanislas Leszczynski, King of Poland and father-in-law of Louis XV of France, and named in honor of Ali Baba from *The Arabian Nights*.

A recipe for the dish appears in the original *Times-Picayune Creole Cookbook*, which was first published in 1900, and is considered one of the early Creole cookbooks. It appears less frequently at restaurants and on New Orleans tables, but when it does, its rum-soaked (ideally *rhum*, appellation d'origine contrôlée French island rum) glory adds a delightful alcoholic finish to any meal.

In this version, the cake is a very simple, very lean dough; the magic is in the rum syrup that completely soaks them.

BABAS
Softened unsalted
   butter, for greasing
2 large eggs, at room
   temperature
½ cup sugar
Scant 1 cup self-rising
   flour, sifted
½ teaspoon kosher salt

RUM SYRUP
1½ cups sugar
½ cup dark rum

FOR SERVING
Dark rum (optional)
Whipped cream

1. MAKE THE BABAS: Preheat the oven to 350°F. Generously butter a 4-hole silicone mini Bundt cake mold.

2. In a stand mixer fitted with the whisk, beat the eggs and sugar on medium speed until frothy. Reduce the speed to low, add the flour and salt, and beat to form a smooth batter. Divide the batter equally among the cake molds.

3. Bake until golden and a tester inserted in the center comes out clean, 20 to 25 minutes.

4. Let cool for 10 minutes in the pan before inverting or dislodging the baba cakes. Place them right-side up on a plate or wire rack set over a small baking sheet.

5. MEANWHILE, MAKE THE RUM SYRUP: In a small saucepan, combine the sugar and ½ cup water. Bring to a boil over medium-high heat and cook for a few minutes until the sugar has dissolved and a slightly thickened syrup forms. Remove from the heat and stir in the rum.

6. Pour the syrup over the cooled baba cakes.

7. Serve at room temperature, with a little more rum poured over the cakes, if desired, and whipped cream.

LA COLLE

MAKES 15 TO 20 PIECES

It is difficult for those of us who grew up going to the store for licorice whips, gumdrops, taffy, or mints to imagine a world where candy was made at home or purchased from those who made sweets for sale. La colle harks back to that era. *La colle* simply means "glue" in French, no doubt because the candy would be sticky before it set into its final form. This recipe for a praline-like candy comes complete with the notation that is it a "truly Creole candy."

In fact, it looks a bit like a cross between a praline and peanut brittle. Nut brittles were popular throughout the American South and throughout the African Atlantic world. This recipe may be a derivative of one of those that made its way into the Costa family's recipe file.

While pralines are cooked so that the sugar reaches a certain temperature that allows them to crumble when eaten, the more straightforward cook-and-cool method here creates a softer candy. Brown sugar and cinnamon make for a delicious flavor that further separates these from the butter/sugar/pecan/milk flavor of pralines.

2 tablespoons salted butter

2 pounds dark brown sugar

1 teaspoon ground cinnamon

2 cups pecans halves or pieces

1 teaspoon vanilla extract

1. Line a baking sheet with parchment paper.

2. In a large wide saucepan, melt the butter over medium heat. Stir in the brown sugar until it is thoroughly melted. Add the cinnamon and stir for about 1 minute, until fragrant. Add the pecans and stir until they are fragrant and lightly toasted, about 1 minute.

3. Remove the pan from the heat and stir the vanilla into the brown sugar mixture until it stops sizzling, about 30 seconds.

4. Pour the pecan mixture onto the prepared baking sheet, spreading it in a single layer. Let it cool to room temperature for about 20 minutes before breaking it into pieces.

CHERRY BOUNCE

MAKES 2½ QUARTS

Cherry bounce was a liqueur that was popular in eighteenth- and nineteenth-century America, where it was prepared by infusing alcohol with cherries and adding sugar, but in fact it was certainly available earlier in American history. George Washington allegedly took a canteen of it on a trip in the Allegheny mountains in 1784. In June of 2024, more than two dozen bottles of cherries and berries dating back to at least 1775 were found in the cellars at Mount Vernon—perhaps they were awaiting transformation into cherry bounce. During the Colonial period, cherry bounce was an accepted tipple for ladies to sip. In the mid-nineteenth century, a North Carolina bootlegger named Amos Owens created a version of the liqueur and became known as the Cherry Bounce King. His version was made with whiskey, honey, and cherries. Each household had its own special fillip that was added, whether it was the liquor infused (some used brandy, rum, or even bourbon), or the amount of added sugar, or other ingredients. A notation on Lou's grandmother's recipe says that the Creoles preferred small black cherries. Traditionally, it would have been consumed as a cordial, but now it can be used as a mixer for cocktails as well. For a photo, see page 142.

8 cups fresh cherries, pitted and rinsed

1 (1-liter) bottle vodka or other neutral spirits (about 4¼ cups)

4 pounds sugar (about 9 cups)

1. Fill a sterilized wide-mouth 3-quart jar with the cherries and pour the vodka over them, pressing to cover them completely. Seal and let stand for 2 weeks in a cool place, preferably in the dark.

2. Line a fine-mesh sieve with a double layer of cheesecloth and place over a bowl. Pour in the jar's contents, pressing the fruit to extract all its juices.

3. In a deep saucepan, bring 4 cups water to a full boil. Remove from the heat and gradually add the sugar, stirring gently until it has all dissolved. Let it stand undisturbed for at least 8 hours, until thoroughly cooled.

4. In a separate container, preferably with a pour spout, mix equal parts of the cherry-infused vodka and the sugar water. Divide the mixture among clean bottles and seal them tightly. Store in a cool place for about 2 months before serving.

A BIBULOUS LOT
ALCOHOL IN EUROPEAN AND AMERICAN CULTURE

It is astonishing for most Americans to read just how much alcohol was consumed in the year of the formation of the Republic. It has been estimated that the Founding Fathers (and mothers) consumed nearly *three times* as much alcohol as today's Americans, much of it in the form of hard cider and beer as well as fortified wines like Madeira, sherry, and port. Fortified wines could survive the sea voyage to the colonies and some, like Madeira, even improved from the rocking of the boats. Washington was not only a fan of Madeira, which was ordered by the pipe (a pipe is 156 gallons!), he was also noted to have been a bon vivant. On one particularly alcoholic night, he ordered fifty-four bottles of Madeira, sixty bottles of claret, as well as seven full bowls of punch and paid for their consumption by his friends and associates.

Washington was also mindful of the commercial possibilities of spirits in Colonial America, and some of his fields were turned over to the cultivation of grains, especially rye, for that purpose. In 1797, he established a distillery at Mount Vernon under the direction of a Scotsman aided by six enslaved workers, and by 1799, the year of his death, Washington's distillery produced 11,000 gallons of spirits for commercial sale. Thomas Jefferson, the oenophile, ordered wine from Europe and attempted to establish vineyards in Virginia. Jefferson's vineyards were not successful; he probably never made a Monticello wine. (Ironically, in the twenty-first century, with modern methods used to control black rot and phylloxera, Virginia wines have become highly accepted in the world.)

Taverns and tavern culture were important parts of Colonial America, especially British Colonial America. They served as post offices, meeting spots, community centers, courts, and more. In them, all manner of switchels, shrubs, whiskeys, and drinks that were the beginning of the country's cocktail culture were consumed. While it may seem unusual to say this, drinking in taverns was not only a pleasant way to pass the time, but also a possible way of saving one's life. Water was often tainted in those days and carried not only parasites, but also all manner of diseases, such as smallpox and more. Drinking fermented or distilled beverages may not seem like a healthful way of staying hydrated today, but we don't have to worry much about lockjaw from a glass of water.

Women drank milder beverages, like hard cider and homemade cordials such as cherry bounce. Even the children drank, usually hard cider or beer, but they were often diluted and enhanced with molasses.

The mention of molasses reminds us that one of the other of the foremost beverages of the early era of the country was rum, like molasses, a by-product of sugar production. Men drank on average seven shots of it a day.

AFRICAN AMERICANS

The forced removal of Africans from our homelands, our enslavement, and our subsequent subjugation is a crime that the United States is only just beginning to acknowledge, and from which the country has yet to heal. The magnitude and scale of the violation is unfathomable and there are really no words that can suitably define it. What we do know is that in the formative years of this country's existence, an extraordinary proportion of the agricultural and domestic work was unpaid, forced labor by those Africans and their descendants. Through this uncompensated—and more often than not unacknowledged—work, the Africans had therefore an incalculable influence on many of America's agricultural systems, manners, and especially on much of the country's food.

Subsequent mixing and mingling of bloods among not only those of African descent but also of their descendants with Europeans and Native Americans means that it is very difficult to trace bloodlines, and consequently the specific origin points and cultures of most African Americans. In many cases we are the living embodiment of the American braid. The "one drop" laws of the southern United States created "African Americans" regardless of the cultures that may have gone into the mix. So it is difficult to know—up until today's DNA tests—if one is Wolof or Yoruba, Kikongo or Fon, from Senegal, from Côte d'Ivoire, or from Angola. The continent surrendered its children from those groups, those places, and beyond. They came with, in their hands, hearts, and heads, recipes and cooking techniques, agricultural, technological, and culinary know-how that became a part of the heritage of their children and their descendants in the country that would become the United States and added their own African flair to the country's food. Because of the Africans' and their descendants' forced divorce from their motherland, and the virtual impossibility of tracing bloodlines and defining specific culinary inheritances, this section will instead look at three elements that influence the cooking of Africans as it forms a part of the American braid: migration, innovation, and regionalism.

Most who were kidnapped and forcibly brought to this country were from the western and central parts of the African continent. While specific foodways are difficult to determine because of unknown and varying points of departure and arrival, it is still possible to make a few general assumptions that should be accepted with the very large grain of salt that should accompany any generality.

American folklorist and anthropologist William Bascom wrote in a landmark 1951 article, "Yoruba Cooking," that in Western Africa the Yoruba people had five principle culinary techniques developed for cooking over open flame:

1. Boiling in water or steaming in leaves
2. Frying in deep oil
3. Toasting beside the fire or in live embers
4. Roasting in the fire
5. Baking in hot ashes

These techniques, based on the use of a three-rock stove, can pretty much be assumed to have been in use throughout the African continent with some variations. They can also be assumed to have traversed the Atlantic and formed the bedrock of much of African American cooking. Ingredients ranged widely, as did climate zones from the Sahel to the forest regions, but okra was known, and millet, true yams, sorghum, and rice were used. Beers were brewed, palm wines were consumed, and the continent fed itself lavishly. Some of the continent's ingredients, like okra and watermelons, made their way into the food of our nascent nation. Others, like peanuts, took a circuitous path from the southern part of the western hemisphere to the north via the African continent; and still others, like true yams, remained in linguistic memory, contributing to confusion that still lasts centuries later. (See page 162 for more.)

Because of the tortuous history of the African diaspora in what would become the United States, the chapter discussing our contributions to the American braid must, of necessity, take a different form than the others. Origin points are mainly unknown, and known ancestors are few. As I spoke with my friends about this section, I was struck by a multiplicity of threads that went into the African American experience. We—for this part of the American braid is deeply personal—did with food what we have done with almost everything that we touched. We improvised, and through that improvisation, we created something else: something different, something better, something truly American. It is what we did with music to produce jazz, the blues, rap, spirituals, and hip-hop. It's how we bend and change language to create the slang that becomes part of mainstream everyday speech. And how we have revolutionized virtually all aspects of American cultural life. This section of *Braided Heritage* will therefore look at African American food through three lenses: that of migration from the South to beyond; that of a strictly *Northern* point of view, a story largely untold; and that of improvisation and innovation.

I spoke first with Dr. Leni Sorensen, a culinary scholar, who worked for decades as scholar-in-residence at Monticello, Thomas Jefferson's plantation in Virginia. She speaks of migration, of her family's journey to California from Louisiana, and of the racial and cultural mixing that took place in her immediate family.

Wanting to remind the world that all African Americans are not Southerners, nor products of the Great Migration, I spoke next with Abigail Rosen McGrath, who has family with no Southern roots. She evinces Northern foodways that in some ways seem more British than those of English-descended Kit Bennett.

Finally, I spoke with Charlotte Lyons, who, as the food editor of *Ebony* magazine, helped to define African American food. I asked her to take some of the classic African American dishes, offer the traditional recipe, and then to come up with a contemporary twist in homage to the innovation and improvisation for which African Americans have always been noted.

QUESTING SOUL

LENI SORENSEN, PhD

The year has long faded from memory, but I met Leni Sorensen at one of the early Southern Foodways Alliance's symposia. At least I think that's the case. I might have met Leni at a hearth cooking convention at Old Salem, North Carolina. Or maybe it was when she reached out to try to connect me with some people in Roanoke who might be related to me. Wherever we met, it was friendship at first sight, based on a common bonding over a mutual love of food and history. At the time, Leni was working as the African American research historian at Monticello, the plantation estate of Thomas Jefferson; a fascinating position that involved equal measures intellectual curiosity, academic research, and practical knowledge. After all, she had not only to understand the history and background of some of the dishes prepared by James Hemings, Jefferson's renowned, enslaved chef, but she also had to be able to prepare them in the hearth where he'd cooked them. And that, while wearing a long skirt that could go up in flames at any moment. She had to live in this century while fully understanding the exigencies of the past.

Insatiably curious, Leni is always questioning and always adventuring. She has a wicked sense of humor, was at one point in her life a homesteader and at another a folk singer who performed on the *Ed Sullivan Show* at least three times. She seems to be in constant motion, and is a voluble talker, larding her conversation with enough profanity to make a sailor blush, but somehow at the same time never offending. In the intervening decades, she earned a PhD in American Studies from William & Mary and has retired from Monticello.

Now, Dr. Sorensen resides in rural Virginia and is teaching home provisioning. Leni's pages on social media abound with images of her canning staggering amounts of homegrown tomatoes, or getting ready to dress a haunch of venison in her rustic, but very well-equipped kitchen.

Although today Leni is a wildcrafting, foraging country woman, her life has had enough twists and turns for a country road. She grew up in urban Los Angeles, a product of the Creole diaspora. As she puts it,

I was born at a time when my parents couldn't marry, even in California . . . [interracial marriage] wasn't legal until 1948. My dad was Black, my mother was white. I've lived all over and after my mother and biological dad divorced, my mother was married several times. And so it wasn't like I was raised in a Black community. But I've always been aware—in a cynical way—of the "one drop" concept. So, I just figured rather than go through a big bunch of these issues, of "what are you, what are you," as a kid, I would just kind of jerk that rug out under them and just call myself Black.

Her background was varied and her influences—cultural and culinary—were just as varied. She recalls that her culinary landscape was diverse. There was traditional Jewish food from Jewish friends and her mother's beloved delicatessens, Mexican foods that she consumed with her friends in San Diego County, the Chinese food that abounded in California, and the African American food that she learned to cook from her stepfather:

He was from Algiers, Louisiana, born in 1914. His father drove the wagon for the white postmaster to take the mail all over the southern parish below Algiers. He was gone away from home a lot. And so Daddy left school in the third grade to take care of his four younger siblings. And in that context, he learned to cook, probably from the surrounding women in the neighborhood. I never quite knew—he wasn't a very voluble kind of person—how he learned how to cook decent food to feed those little children. His repertoire is what I learned, and then what I cooked: red beans and rice and collard greens and green beans and sweet potatoes and corn bread and, you know, real basic. There was always rice, really a lot of rice.

Leni also learned to cook at a very early age, because while her mother really loved to eat and encouraged her to try all kinds of foods, she didn't really enjoy cooking. A dyed-in-the-

wool red liberal in California in the 1950s, with a husband who enjoyed cooking, she didn't have to. And so, for Leni, there would be church dinners with her father.

He would pick me up and we would go to all the local Black churches in San Diego. Little tiny storefront churches, and real churches with a real church building and a ladies' auxiliary and all of that. But they would all be out on the sidewalk and they'd have fried fish and barbecued chicken, greens and the whole standard kind of fancy dinner array.

Then, there was also the rustic, produce-centered cooking that came from her birth father's relatives, who lived on a farm. From this omnivorous universe, Leni learned to eat the world: "As a young girl, I was a greedy child: a skinny greedy child who never had enough. I loved meat and salt."

California was only the beginning of Leni's voracious culinary journey; she lived for the longest period of her life in South Dakota. But, as she attests, "I'm definitely a descendant of Southerners, my Texan grandfather, and my Alabama-born grandmother and, my stepfather and other people, who formed how I cook. They were all from all over the South." The South followed her, as it did with most of the children of the Great Migration, which began in the late nineteenth century and took six million African Americans from the Deep South and spread them and their foodways across the country.

Leni's family history and her journey around the country are oh-so-personal, and yet serves to illuminate the complexity of trying to define any one African American journey.

DADDY ROBERT'S FRICASSÉE CHICKEN OR PORK

SERVES 3 TO 4

This recipe produces a dense, rich stew that is particularly tasty when served over white rice. The ingredients are not lavish, but the technique of browning the meat well, and then creating a toasty brown roux, provides great depth to the flavor of the gravy. You may choose whether to use chicken or pork.

It is interesting that Leni's Daddy Robert was from Louisiana, as this recipe for a fricassée is quite like the one from John Barbry's Tunica-Biloxi folks (see page 60), with the key distinction that this one is richly roux-thickened, whereas Barbry's is looser and brothier. As Barbry informed us, the braid runs deep with the connections between the Native peoples and the French, and also between the Native peoples and the African Americans.

If the fricassée is served in the summer, it's great with Leni's High-Summer Tomato Salad (page 168).

3 pounds bone-in, skin-on chicken thighs, or 3 pounds bone-in pork chops, cut 1½ inches thick

½ teaspoon garlic powder

1¼ teaspoons sweet paprika

Kosher salt and freshly ground black pepper

1⅓ cups all-purpose flour

3 tablespoons lard or vegetable oil

2 cups hot water, or as needed

Cooked white rice, for serving (optional)

1. Pat the chicken thighs or pork chops dry with paper towels. In a small bowl, stir together the garlic powder, 1 teaspoon of the paprika, 1½ teaspoons salt, and ¼ teaspoon pepper. Season the meat all over with the spice mixture.

2. In a shallow dish, stir together 1 cup of the flour, the remaining ¼ teaspoon paprika, ½ teaspoon salt, and ½ teaspoon pepper.

3. In a Dutch oven or cast-iron skillet, heat the lard over medium-high heat until shimmering.

4. Meanwhile, coat each chicken thigh or pork chop in the flour mixture, shaking off excess.

5. Working in batches, add the chicken or pork to the Dutch oven and cook until nicely browned all over but not cooked through, 6 to 7 minutes per side. Transfer to a platter, reserving the drippings in the pan.

6. Reduce the heat to medium. Whisk the remaining ⅓ cup flour into the Dutch oven to form a smooth roux. When it is at least the color of peanut butter but not darker than a penny, whisk in 1 cup of the hot water to make a thin gravy. Check the seasoning, adding salt and pepper a pinch at a time.

7. Return the chicken or pork to the Dutch oven, nestling the pieces into the gravy. Add some or all of the remaining hot water to make sure the sides of the meat are covered, but you don't have to fully submerge the meat.

8. Reduce the heat to low, partially cover, and simmer until the meat is very tender and the gravy is rich, 1 to 1½ hours.

9. If the gravy is too reduced, add some water to thin it back out. Taste and adjust the seasoning if necessary. Serve with rice, if desired.

TURKEY AND GRAVY

SERVES 10 TO 12

Back in the days, when Thanksgiving was a holiday that was widely celebrated entirely without thought of the broken promises and carnage its history actually symbolizes, turkeys were less common and only seasonally available. Leni remembers, "As was the custom at the time, Daddy roasted his bird whole and stuffed full of dressing at the big cavity and at the neck, with the openings sewed closed." She continues:

> Over the long years I changed over to my method: On Wednesday morning I spatchcock the bird, removing the backbone and neck, deboning the whole breast cavity along with the thigh bones and wing tips. I bake the stuffing in a separate pan.
>
> Finally, throw away that dumb plastic temp thingy—either use a real thermometer or learn how to wiggle the leg bone to test for doneness. If it wiggles back and forth, it's done!

Spatchcocking the bird is when you cut it open on the back side and splay it out, opening it up flat, like laying a book down on its pages. This takes care of some of the usual problems of juicy legs and dry breast and results in a much more quickly cooked—and more *evenly* cooked—bird overall. The dark and light meat of Leni's cooked bird are succulent, aromatic with garlic and paprika.

TURKEY

- 4 teaspoons garlic powder
- 4 teaspoons sweet paprika
- 2 tablespoons kosher salt
- 2 teaspoons freshly ground black pepper
- 12- to 14-pound turkey, giblets and neck removed
- 8 tablespoons (1 stick) unsalted butter, at room temperature

GRAVY

- 4 cups chicken stock, turkey stock, or vegetable broth
- ½ cup all-purpose flour
- Kosher salt and freshly ground black pepper

1. **PREP THE TURKEY:** Position an oven rack in the lower third of the oven and preheat the oven to 300°F.

2. In a medium bowl, mix together the garlic powder, paprika, salt, and pepper.

3. Place the bird breast-side down. Using heavy kitchen shears, cut along either side of the backbone; you should be able to find a more cuttable line along the spine where the bones connect. Reserve the backbone for stock or discard it.

4. Turn the turkey breast-side up while "opening" the back so that it sits a bit like a tent. Using the heels of your hands and your own weight, press down firmly on the peak of the tent to flatten the breastbone.

5. Turn the spatchcocked bird skin-side down. Use half the spice mixture to rub into the meat. Turn it breast-side up again, slather generously with the butter, and season with the remaining spice mixture.

6. Transfer the turkey to a roasting pan and tuck under the wings. (A sheet pan with a wire rack works well.)

7. Slow-roast the turkey until an instant-read thermometer registers 160°F when inserted in the thickest part of the breast and 170°F in the thickest part of thigh, about 2½ hours. The skin should be crisped and nicely browned; if it could use some more help, turn the broiler on and broil the top of the skin.

8. Let the turkey rest in the pan for at least 30 minutes and up to 1 hour. Transfer the turkey to a cutting board and tent loosely with aluminum foil, keeping the drippings in the pan (for the gravy).

9. **MAKE THE GRAVY:** In a large saucepan, heat the stock or broth over medium heat until steaming-hot.

10. Place the roasting pan with drippings across two burners over medium heat. When the drippings start to simmer, gradually whisk in the flour. Whisk or stir for 3 to 5 minutes, dislodging any browned bits until the mixture (roux) is golden brown.

11. Add ladlefuls of the hot stock to the pan, stirring after each addition. Do this until you've thinned the roux to a very thick, smooth gravy consistency. Then scrape the roux mixture back into the saucepan with the rest of the stock.

12. Season the gravy, starting with ½ teaspoon salt and ¼ teaspoon pepper. Cook over medium-low heat for 30 minutes, whisking or stirring occasionally, until reduced and thickened. Taste and adjust the seasoning with salt and pepper as needed.

13. Serve the turkey with gravy alongside.

TURKEYS

Turkeys are native to this hemisphere. Two different species of wild turkeys were independently domesticated in the Americas more than two thousand years ago: one breed in the Southwestern United States by the Anasazi, and another in Mexico by the Aztecs. There were once an estimated ten million wild turkeys in the United States, but with the destruction of their forest habitat, their numbers declined. In New England, where they once had roamed free in great numbers, they had to be repopulated by importing wild turkeys from New York State. Those who have only seen the top-heavy domesticated turkeys, bred for breast meat, nearly tipping over, would almost not recognize it as a relative of the sleek, wily wild animal that can once again be found on some New England roads.

The musical *1776* popularized a rumor that Benjamin Franklin wanted the turkey to be the national symbol of the United States instead of the predatory bald eagle. He didn't; the piece that is often cited in support of that assertion was a satirical one. However, Franklin did defend the turkey, saying it was, "a much more respectable Bird, and withal a true original Native of America. . . . He is besides, though a little vain and silly, a Bird of Courage." Turkeys are in fact quite remarkable, with excellent eyesight and the ability to fly. Anyone who has been on the end of a charge by an aggressive turkey would certainly agree that while they may be a bit dim, they do indeed have courage . . . though they also make for very good eating indeed at holiday times.

CORN BREAD STUFFING

SERVES 6 TO 8

Stuffings and dressings can be difficult enough to negotiate, especially if guests come from different parts of the country. This corn bread stuffing is as Southern as it gets. I have Thanksgiving dinner at some friends' house where they often make two different stuffings: a corn bread one for the Southern guests, and an oyster one for the Creole guests to stop the arguments—but that's another story. Leni's is as stuffing should be, not too soggy or too dry so that all can savor the slight grainy crunch of the corn bread, with enough taste to counterpoint the turkey. The corn bread stuffing goes beautifully with the turkey and gravy recipe on page 156 and together they would be a proud addition to any Thanksgiving table.

2 (8.5-ounce) boxes Jiffy Corn Muffin Mix, or a corn bread mix of your choice

1 teaspoon kosher salt, plus more to taste

2 teaspoons freshly ground black pepper

½ cup (packed) fresh sage, chopped

4 tablespoons (½ stick) salted butter, at room temperature

4 celery stalks, finely chopped

2 medium yellow onions, cut into ¼-inch dice

2½ cups turkey stock, chicken stock, or vegetable broth

1. At least 1 day in advance, prepare and bake the corn muffin mix according to the package directions, adding the salt, pepper, and sage. Cool in its pan set on a wire rack for 1 hour.

2. Turn the cooled corn bread out of its pan and cut into ½-inch cubes. Let them sit, uncovered, in a large bowl for at least 1 day; this will ensure they are dried.

3. Preheat the oven to 375°F. Use 2 tablespoons of the butter to grease a 9 × 13-inch baking dish.

4. In a Dutch oven, melt the remaining 2 tablespoons butter over medium-high heat. Add the celery and onions and cook until the onions begin to brown, about 8 minutes.

5. Add this to the bowl of corn bread cubes, toss to mix well, and transfer the mixture to the baking dish. Add ladlefuls of the turkey stock, gently folding with a spatula to ensure even distribution. Taste and add more salt if necessary.

6. Bake until the stuffing is crusty on the edges, it should be scoopable but still moist, 1 hour to 1 hour 10 minutes. Serve warm.

OVEN-BAKED YAMS

SERVES 8 TO 12

Baking in the ashes of a fire is one of the culinary techniques that anthropologist William Bascom says was a part of Yoruba practice and it can, by extension, be thought to have been widely done throughout the African continent. It is certainly a technique that would have been used in the historical kitchens where Leni cooked.

Although in times past the so-called yams would have been roasted in the embers of a fireplace until very soft and caramelized, these, done in the oven, are almost as good, albeit without the slightly smoky undertone of the fire-roasted ones.

The word "yam" is a worthy subject for a short dissertation as well. Suffice it to say here that these "yams" are not yams at all, but rather sweet potatoes. In brief, true yams are the edible tubers of perennial herbaceous vines of the *Dioscoreaceae* genus. They have a rough, dark brown skin and a dry flesh that is a bit like a white potato in texture. They are also usually sold in pieces, as they can grow up to seven feet in length and weigh as much as one hundred pounds. Sweet potatoes, which are what is used in this recipe, are members of the *Ipomea* genus and are related to morning glories. They have smooth skins and moist flesh that may be orange, white, or purple and are considerably smaller than true yams. They are New World tubers.

The cultural importance of the true yam is such that variants of the word *yam*—or *nyam*—mean "to taste" or "to eat" in several West African languages. In the Gullah language of the Geechee/Gullah Lowcountry in the United States, and in Jamaican patois, the verb "to eat" is *nyam*, as in "food for to nyam." It is not inconceivable then, given the cultural importance of the true yam, that early enslaved Africans gave the tuber that they *had* the name of the tuber that they *knew*, and began to call sweet potatoes "yams."

8 large orange-fleshed sweet potatoes, scrubbed well

3 tablespoons vegetable oil

Butter, for serving (optional)

Kosher salt and black pepper (optional)

1. Position an oven rack in the lower third of the oven and preheat the oven to 400°F. Line a sheet pan with aluminum foil.

2. Using a sharp knife, pierce each sweet potato 8 to 10 times. Use the oil to rub the sweet potatoes all over and place them on the pan.

3. Roast until the skins loosen, the flesh is fork-tender, and some natural sugars have caramelized on the foil, 1 to 1½ hours.

4. Serve hot, plain or with butter, salt, and pepper.

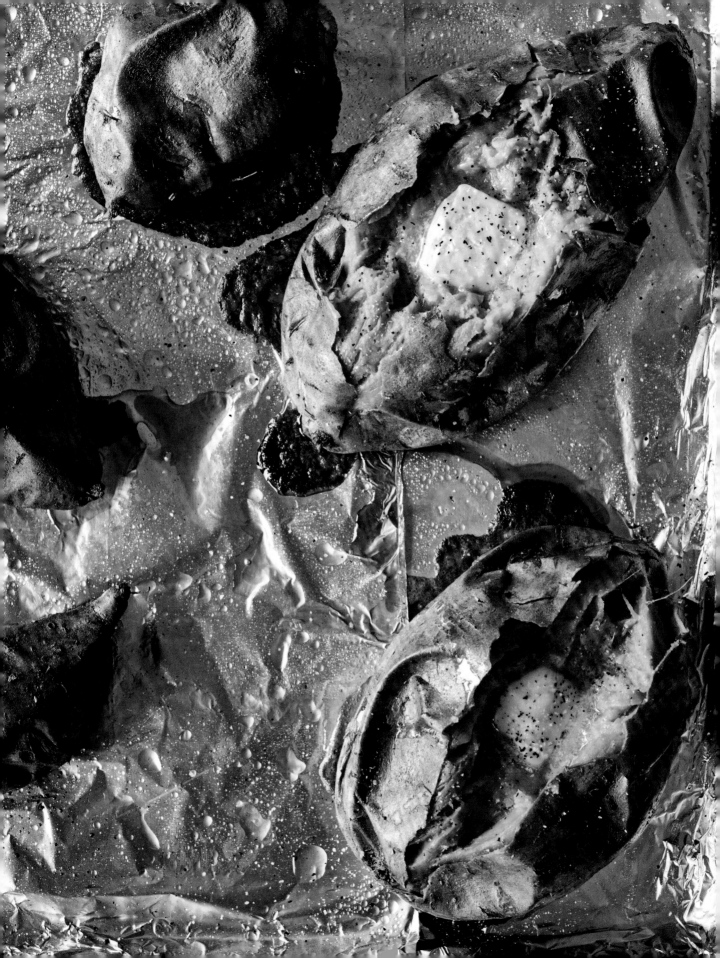

RED BEANS AND RICE

SERVES 6 TO 8

Red beans and rice is an iconic dish of southern Louisiana and found in all communities, including the Creole and Cajun ones. Jazz icon Louis Armstrong loved them so much that he signed his letters, "red beans and ricely yours."

While many recipes feature a base of the Holy Trinity of onion, celery, and green pepper, and are loaded with pork products like sausage or ham bones, Leni's is vegetarian. She claims it's modest and says, "I make no spectacular claims for my version of this Louisiana favorite." She does, however, finish her bowl at the table with the crunch, flavor, and freshness of chopped or sliced onion, jalapeños, and summer-ripe tomato. I find Leni's vegetarian version is wonderfully versatile, and is a saucy and satisfying accompaniment to everything from roasts to fried dishes.

Since the ingredients speak for themselves here, try this with high-quality, flavorful red beans. In Louisiana, the typical brand of choice is Camellia. Alternately, select an heirloom variety, from a national artisanal brand such as Rancho Gordo.

1 pound dried red beans (2 cups)

1 tablespoon garlic powder

1 tablespoon chili powder

Kosher salt

FOR SERVING

2 cups cooked Carolina Gold rice

1 medium white onion, chopped

1 or more jalapeños, cut crosswise into ¼-inch slices

1 large tomato, chopped

1. A day before you cook the beans, spread them out on a sheet pan and gently shake to find and discard any broken beans, rocks, or dirt. Repeat two more times.

2. In a large pot or Dutch oven, combine the sorted beans and enough water to cover by 2 to 3 inches. Let soak, covered, overnight or for at least 8 hours.

3. Drain and rinse the beans with cool water. Return the beans to the pot and add enough water to cover them by 5 inches, at least 8 cups. Bring to a boil over high heat and cook for 10 minutes, skimming off any foam that forms on top.

4. Reduce the heat to medium-low, a gentle simmer. Add the garlic powder, chili powder, and ½ teaspoon salt. It will be underseasoned for now. Cover and cook until the beans are tender and the liquid has begun to thicken. The cooking time can vary with the age of the beans, so start checking at 45 minutes, but they might cook for 60 or 90 minutes or more. Check every 15 minutes or so, adding water if necessary to keep them well submerged. (Very old beans may eventually cook through and begin to burst, but may not feel entirely smooth.)

5. When the beans are nearly done, adjust the seasoning, especially adding salt; it should taste flavorful enough to be served with plain rice.

6. Divide the beans and some of their liquid among individual bowls and top with spoonfuls of the rice. Pass the chopped onion, jalapeño, and tomato at the table to top each serving.

AUNT MARY'S SUMMER VEGETABLE DISH

SERVES 8

Each year Leni's aunt Mary, the youngest sister of her grandmother Maude Florence Clark Bedney, waited for the first crop of all the ingredients in this recipe to be ready: new potatoes, the first tomatoes of the season, small green beans, and young onions. She would celebrate by making this, a layered stew seasoned first with smoky bacon.

Many folks who think of African American food as being bereft of fresh vegetables might believe that Leni's West Coast upbringing is driving her love of seasonal bounty. However, the truth is that for many African Americans, garden plots—be they small urban ones or large family farms—are also very much a part of the African American culinary journey. Aunt Mary and her fresh Alabama vegetable dish speak to that tradition. Serve this with corn bread or Corn Pone (page 169).

1. In a cast-iron Dutch oven or other heavy pot, lay the bacon in a single layer and cook over medium heat until crisped. Pour off the fat, leaving the bacon in place.

2. Arrange the onions on top of the bacon and season with salt and pepper. Layer on the rest of the vegetables in this order (overlapping is okay), seasoning each layer with salt and pepper as you go: potatoes, tomatoes, haricots verts.

3. Add ¼ cup water, cover, and bring to a simmer over medium-high heat. Reduce the heat to medium-low and cook until the vegetables can be pierced easily with a sharp knife, 20 to 25 minutes. Without stirring, check the vegetables often and add more water to avoid scorching. Remove from the heat.

4. Let sit, covered, for 10 minutes before serving so the juices are absorbed and the vegetables are tender.

6 slices bacon

1½ pounds onions (ideally tender, young ones), cut into ½-inch-thick rounds

Kosher salt and freshly ground black pepper

1½ pounds Yukon Gold or new potatoes, peeled and cut into ½-inch-thick rounds

1 pound haricots verts or tender green beans

1½ pounds tomatoes (3 or 4 medium), cut into ½-inch-thick rounds

LENI'S HIGH-SUMMER TOMATO SALAD

SERVES 4 TO 6

As with Aunt Mary's Summer Vegetable Dish (page 166), this recipe shows a deep African American love of fresh produce. Leni has much to say about this recipe, so I leave it to her:

I have a personal rule about this salad. No matter how tempted, I never make it till I have homegrown tomatoes from my own garden. For those of you who do not garden, aim to get very fresh tomatoes from your local farmers' market. And, the rest of the ingredients must also be as fresh and local as you can arrange. NEVER make this salad with store tomatoes, please. Notice that "never" is in caps and underlined!

Consequently, tomato salad is a mid- to late-summer dish; the epitome of seasonal. Where I garden, the ingredients are only available fresh, all at the same time, in early August through September. If you have a longer season, you are certainly lucky, and can start enjoying this delicious salad earlier than I can! I envy you.

- 2 pounds tomatoes, cut into ½-inch cubes
- 3 medium cucumbers, diced
- 1 small sweet onion (white, red, or Vidalia), cut into ¼-inch dice
- 6 mini red and yellow sweet peppers, cut into ¼-inch dice (optional)
- 1 or 2 large garlic cloves, thinly sliced (optional)
- 1 teaspoon kosher salt, plus more to taste
- ¼ teaspoon freshly ground black pepper, plus more to taste
- 2 tablespoons olive oil
- 2 teaspoons cider vinegar
- 1 teaspoon balsamic vinegar
- ¼ cup (packed) fresh basil leaves, thinly sliced
- 2 tablespoons finely chopped fresh parsley
- 1 tablespoon finely chopped fresh chives

1. In a large bowl, toss together the tomatoes, cucumbers, onion, mini peppers (if using), garlic (if using), salt, and black pepper. Add the olive oil and both vinegars, stirring gently until just combined. Taste and adjust the seasoning with salt and black pepper as needed.

2. Just before serving, add the basil, parsley, and chives and toss lightly to distribute. Serve immediately.

CORN PONE

MAKES 6 TO 8 CORN PONES

Leni's paternal grandmother, Maude Florence Clark Bedney (born in 1889 in Boligee, Alabama, and died in 1993 in Los Angeles, California) taught Leni to make this pone when she was eight years old, informing her that *pone* is the Ojibwe word for "little corn cake." In many parts of the South they are also called ashcakes, Johnnie cakes, hearth cakes, or hot water corn bread. Johnny cakes, sometimes called journey cakes or hoecakes, are a type of flat corn bread that is cooked into a thick pancake (see page 172 for Abigail McGrath's version). They are eaten all along the Atlantic Coast of North America, from Canada through the Caribbean. The bread is most likely Native American in origin, but has been connected with African Americans since the late eighteenth century. Leni's are essentially pan-fried unleavened corn bread cakes, quick to make, and wonderful with butter and a syrup.

Again, as with Daddy Robert's Fricassée Chicken (page 155), it is interesting to note just how the culinary threads braid early in the Southeast. Here, though, the African Americans are making cakes with Native American corn, while the Native Americans in John Barbry's community are making Pan-Fried Galettes (page 55), using almost the same cooking techniques but with European wheat! For a photo, see these served with Daddy Robert's Fricassée Chicken on page 154.

2 cups stone-ground cornmeal

Kosher salt

1 cup hot water (but not boiling), plus more as needed

Vegetable oil or lard, for pan-frying

Butter, for serving

Honey, sorghum, molasses, or maple syrup, for serving

1. In a bowl, stir together the cornmeal and several pinches of salt. Gradually stir in just enough of the hot water to form a thick dough. Taste a pinch of it to see if the dough is sufficiently seasoned and add salt if it isn't. Cover the bowl with a clean kitchen towel and let it rest for 15 to 20 minutes. During that time, check to see if the dough has dried out and add more hot water as needed. You want it to be solid, but pliable so it holds its shape when formed.

2. To form the corn pones, place a generous portion of the dough in the palm of one hand and use the middle three fingers of your other hand to press it into a patty. Each one should be about palm size, 3 inches across and ½ inch thick.

3. Line a platter with paper towels and have nearby. In a cast-iron skillet or griddle, add enough oil or lard to come up ¼ inch or so and heat over medium heat until it shimmers.

4. Working in batches to not crowd the pan, carefully add the pones to the hot oil and cook until golden brown on the first side, 3 or 4 minutes. Flip and cook until browned on the second side and cooked through, another 3 or 4 minutes. Drain briefly on the paper towels.

5. Serve hot, with butter and honey, sorghum, molasses, or maple syrup.

6. Pones freeze well and can be easily reheated in the microwave or toaster.

ADVENTUROUS DAUGHTER OF THE NORTH

ABIGAIL ROSEN McGRATH

Abigail Rosen McGrath and I should have been childhood friends, and be able to boast of girlhoods spent together frolicking in the sand at the beaches on Martha's Vineyard, or meeting for drinks in West Village coffeehouses. We share no such memories, but have built a fair number of recent ones as summer friends on the Vineyard, where she runs Renaissance House, a twenty-three-year-old writer's retreat that is a refuge for creatives who might not otherwise have time or energy to produce. We met only a decade and a half ago when I was asked by a mutual friend to read one of her mother's poems at a fundraiser. Needless to say, it was friendship at first glance.

In our conversations, I discovered that Abigail has had enough life experiences to fill at least two full miniseries. First, I learned that she was a copywriter at the global advertising firm Doyle Dane Bernbach in the *Mad Men* days when women, not to mention African American ones, were very rare indeed. Then, she allowed that she'd worked as a mannequin at the Folies Bergères in Paris and as a solo dancer at the Crazy Horse Saloon. A single mom raising two boys, she often worked three jobs simultaneously. Someone whispered to me that, back in New York, she appeared in Broadway and off-Broadway shows, wrote and produced a

prize-winning film, and was an Andy Warhol Tub Girl! Over dinner one evening, she confessed to an entrepreneurial bent and admitted that she owned the hat check concession at the Village Vanguard and at Max's Kansas City, where Lou Reed wrote about her in the iconic song "Walk on the Wild Side" ("... and the colored girls go do dee do dee do dee do dee do"). She also had a bread company that sold bread to Times Square restaurants and boxed lunches in Central Park. The most recent revelation to me was that she and her late husband, Tony McGrath, were the founders of the legendary Off Center Theatre, which produced experimental plays and street theater all around New York City and served as a launchpad for such actors as John Leguizamo, Christine Baranski, and F. Murray Abraham. And I suspect that there's more behind all of that!

As our friendship grew, I was thrilled when she asked me if I would read from my work in one of the evening programs at Renaissance House. My connection with the retreat allowed me to become one of her island co-conspirators and brought other creative adventures to my island summers.

Abigail's almost exclusively Northern upbringing represents an often-unacknowledged aspect of African American food: that of foodways of families who had little if any connection to the American South. Many who migrated to other areas of the country maintained culinary connections with the South no matter how great the geographical distance. Creole foodways were maintained in California as attested to by Leni Sorensen. Period accounts speak of discreet signs in windows in the Midwest and West signaling the arrival of possum or boiled peanuts to tempt palates still attuned to Southern tastes.

However, many of the families who were rooted in the North maintained differing foodways. Abigail was raised in New York City by a very bluestocking community of women that included her mother, poet Helene Johnson, and her aunt, author Dorothy West: both superstars of the Harlem Renaissance. West's 1995 novel, *The Wedding,* which was transformed into a 1998 television film starring Halle Berry, was based on Abigail's own wedding. A genteel poverty prevailed in her female-centered family, as did a hewing to Northern and more European-facing foodways that included such dishes as chowders, sardine sandwiches, and brown breads. She states:

> *I grew up on fish cakes and baked beans, but it didn't occur to me that it was not a Black dish. I grew up with an identity of being from New England. We were Yankees. Black Yankees, but we didn't see it as anything other than Black Yankees. There was no caste system or judgment on it.*

When I attended my first of the evening sessions at the house, I was simultaneously astonished and delighted to notice that one part of the process of Renaissance House for Abigail was that she is a masterful entertainer who carefully curates each of her meals as though it were a performance. From napkin rings to table-scaping, everything is coordinated and thought through. One evening that I attended, she'd crafted a verse for each of the dinner attendees that spoke to their writing project. Abundance

is a watchword, and her groaning board dinners include multiple meats, several salads, and an array of side dishes and condiments. Her culinary inspirations are wide-ranging, and a meal might include a nod to India or a wink at the South Pacific.

Abigail's culinary inspirations may be international, but her roots, unlike those of many African Americans who hark from the South, remain firmly grounded in the North. She continues:

> *My mother never stepped one foot in the South; she learned to cook from her mother, who left the South as a teenager. When called on to make collard greens, she made them with butter. I finally learned how to make Southern-style collard greens from my father, who, too, was a fourth-generation New Yorker. But I learned to put ham hocks and a little sugar on them and sometimes a little vinegar. The first time that I had hominy grits, I assumed it was cream of wheat and put sugar on them.*

Abigail's identity as a Black Yankee would display itself in her family's foodways and evidences the extraordinary ability of African Americans to adapt. If we lived in the North, we assimilated and ate the predominant foods. The dishes that Abigail selected to share with us celebrate her Yankee roots, and stylistically may ironically seem more "British" in some cases than those of Kit Bennett, a descendant of British colonists in Charleston (see page 102). Likewise, if we lived in the Midwest or the Northwest, we added those foods to our tables as well.

Because of her family's Northern tenure, Abigail ably represents our singular genius at reworking the culinary landscape in which we find ourselves, albeit with the occasional nod to the more traditional African American palate, like the dash of hot sauce in her sardine sandwich!

JOHNNY CAKES

SERVES 2 TO 4

It was my pleasure to be asked to curate the menu at the Sweet Home Café, the restaurant at the Smithsonian National Museum of African American History and Culture, and to later work with chefs Albert Lukas and Jerome Grant on writing the restaurant's cookbook, which was then nominated for a James Beard Award. In doing so, I learned much about the history of American food.

In that book I wrote:

There are many kinds of johnnycakes, sometimes called journey cakes or hoecakes. In the South and up and down the Atlantic Seaboard, they are often a cornmeal flatbread. Native Americans originated these hearty cakes, and some food historians believe the word johnnycake comes from the colonial pronunciation of Shawnee cake.

Today, hoecakes, corn bread, and yes, johnny cakes are an indelible part of the Southern and African American culinary lexicon, but this possible etymology reminds us that the Native peoples' foodways undergird so much of what became American cuisine.

Unlike Leni Sorensen's version called Corn Pone (page 169), this rendition's use of sugar and milk clearly speak to non-Native influence as well. What results is a sweet, hearty pancake that is at home as a side to savory food as it is served with butter and honey, molasses, or syrup.

1 cup medium-grind yellow cornmeal
¼ teaspoon kosher salt
¼ cup (packed) light brown sugar
1 cup boiling water
¼ cup whole milk or evaporated milk
Vegetable oil, as needed

1. In a medium bowl, whisk together the cornmeal, salt, and brown sugar. Add the boiling water and milk, stirring to form a thick, pancake-like batter. It should plop from a spoon.

2. Line a plate with paper towels and place it nearby. In a cast-iron skillet, heat a generous film of vegetable oil over medium heat until it shimmers. Drop (large or small) spoonfuls of batter into the pan. Cook until crisped and browned on the first side, 3 to 4 minutes. Turn them over and cook on the second side until the bottom edges start to brown, another minute or so. Repeat, regreasing the skillet as needed, to use all the batter.

3. Transfer to the paper towels to drain. Serve warm.

SAUTÉED LIVER WITH TOMATOES

SERVES 4

Liver is not something that everyone is fond of, but I am a liver lover and so is Abigail. She notes, "back in the days, it was considered very good for you." Also, as an organ meat, liver was, in her childhood, an inexpensive and therefore accessible cut of meat. "My mother preferred it served the traditional fried/sautéed way, cooked in a cast-iron skillet on the back of the stove."

Liver is rich and deeply flavored. Some love its minerality but others find it a bit overbearing; soaking it in milk is said to smooth out those flavors. (Substituting calf's liver for beef liver also yields a milder taste.) Served browned in butter—take care not to overcook it, lest it become tough, chalky, and even more minerally in flavor—and with its traditional English accompaniment of sautéed onions, it's intensely satisfying. Abigail loves it with sliced, ripe tomatoes dressed with mayonnaise, a sweet-tart counter to the very savory meat.

2 cups whole milk

1 pound beef or calf's liver, trimmed of fat and gristle, and sliced crosswise into ½-inch strips

1 cup all-purpose flour

Kosher salt and freshly ground black pepper

4 tablespoons (½ stick) salted butter

1 large yellow onion, sliced

Sliced very ripe tomatoes, for serving

Mayonnaise (preferably Hellmann's), for serving

1. In a large wide bowl, pour the milk over the liver, pressing to make sure the slices are covered. Soak at room temperature for 30 minutes to 1 hour.

2. Meanwhile, in a shallow baking dish, season the flour with salt and pepper.

3. In a large cast-iron skillet, melt 2 tablespoons of the butter over medium-high heat until slightly bubbling. Add the onion and cook until softened, about 5 minutes. Season with salt and pepper. Transfer to a plate.

4. Remove the liver from the milk and pat dry. Quickly dredge each piece of liver in the flour mixture to coat completely and place on a sheet pan.

5. In the same cast-iron skillet, heat the remaining 2 tablespoons butter over medium-high heat until it is browned. Add the liver in one layer and season with salt. Cook 2 or 3 minutes, flipping once, until golden brown and springy (not stiff) to the touch.

6. Transfer to a platter and top with the cooked onion.

7. Serve with sliced tomatoes with a big dollop of mayonnaise on top.

SALMON POACHED IN MILK

SERVES 6 TO 8

Many folks from the South revel in fish fries, featuring fish like whiting, catfish, and mullet. Salmon, if it appeared at all on the African American table, often showed up as croquettes prepared from canned salmon that was in those days relatively inexpensive. Abigail McGrath and her relatives in the North, however, ate fresh salmon, which they poached in milk and seasoned with a bit of nutmeg. The effect is a mild-flavored dish, with a beautiful silky texture. Be sure to check on the salmon while cooking so that you don't overcook it. You may use a thermometer to ensure your preferred doneness, but when the fish just starts to flake easily if prodded, it's done. Serve this mild, rich fish with a tart salad, bread, and butter.

4 tablespoons (½ stick) salted butter

Kosher salt

1 (4-pound) skin-on salmon fillet (cut in half if too large for the pan)

1 small onion, thinly sliced

¼ teaspoon freshly grated nutmeg

3 cups whole milk, at room temperature

1. Preheat the oven to 275°F.

2. In a 12-inch nonstick skillet, melt 2 tablespoons of the butter over medium-high heat. Season the salmon all over with salt. Add the salmon (working in two batches if necessary) skin-side down and sear until browned, 3 to 5 minutes. Then flip and lightly sear the flesh side until just golden, 1 minute or so. Transfer the salmon to a 9 × 13-inch baking dish, skin-side down.

3. In the same skillet, heat the remaining 2 tablespoons butter over medium heat. Add the onion and nutmeg and cook until the onion is translucent and lightly browned, about 5 minutes.

4. Add the milk to the pan and scrape to pick up any browned bits. Cook until the milk is just starting to simmer. Taste and season with salt, if necessary. Pour the skillet sauce over the salmon so it is completely covered.

5. Transfer to the oven and poach the salmon until it flakes easily, 15 to 20 minutes.

6. Serve hot, spooning the sauce over the fish.

CREAMY CLAM CHOWDER

SERVES 4

This is simply a New England classic, familiar to any and all who have spent time in the region. It's been a must-have on Abigail's table on the Vineyard every summer during clamming season. Then, clams were to be had with a rake, basket, and, of course, a clamming license. Abigail has been known to serve it to the attendees at Renaissance House: the summer writers' residency that she runs in honor of her mother, Helene Johnson, and her aunt, Dorothy West.

The term "chowder" comes from the French term *chaudron*, the vessel in which the soup is traditionally cooked. There are multiple versions of clam chowder: The New York one has tomatoes and is a bit like an Italian minestrone; Clear Broth Clam Chowder (page 27) seems to have been favored by coastal Northeastern Native peoples who of course originally created this soup without dairy, as cows were a colonial import; and this more familiar version, commonly thought of as New England Clam Chowder. It features cream, bacon or salt pork, and potatoes along with the clams. While you can certainly use freshly shucked or steamed clams for this recipe, the use of canned clams—which are already cooked to tenderness—prevents toughness in the clams while the chowder simmers for a while.

3 slices thick-cut bacon, cut into ½-inch pieces

1 pound yellow onions, cut into ½-inch cubes

Kosher salt

Ground white pepper

2 tablespoons all-purpose flour

1 cup bottled clam juice

½ cup dry white wine

¼ cup dry sherry

3 medium Yukon Gold potatoes, scrubbed well and cut into ½-inch cubes

1 bay leaf

1 cup heavy cream

4 (6.5-ounce) cans minced clams, undrained

¼ cup fresh flat-leaf parsley, minced

1. In a Dutch oven, cook the bacon over medium heat until its fat renders and the bacon crisps, about 5 minutes.

2. Add the onions and a few pinches of salt and white pepper and cook until softened and translucent, about 5 minutes.

3. Stir in the flour to coat the bacon and onions and cook for about 1 minute until everything looks a bit matte. Whisk in the clam juice, wine, and sherry and bring to a simmer. Add the potatoes and bay leaf. Increase the heat to medium-high and bring to a boil. Reduce to a simmer and cook uncovered for 8 to 10 minutes or until the potatoes are just starting to soften.

4. Stir in the cream, clams and their juice, and parsley. (Reserve a few pinches of parsley for garnish.) Bring to a simmer, then reduce the heat to medium-low and simmer for 15 minutes to meld the flavors and finish cooking the potatoes.

5. Discard the bay leaf. Taste and season with salt and pepper. Serve hot, garnished with the reserved parsley.

SARDINE SANDWICHES

SERVES 2

Abigail's New York City past comes with the question, "Silvercup or Wonder Bread?" Both companies had bakeries in New York from which they purveyed the pillowy soft white bread of Abigail's and my childhood. She continues, "That was the only decision-making factor. Whichever bread was chosen, it had to be toasted. Only sardines packed in oil were around in those days, no mustard or other fancy stuff, so the other major question was . . . did the can have enough sardines for two sandwiches?"

While the sandwiches are quite tasty, back in the day, they often brought wrinkled noses when packed for school lunches because they do smell strongly of fish and the briny deep. Today, high-quality sardines, often from Portugal or Spain, are available in gourmet or specialty shops, and increasingly in groceries. They are way fancier than the ones we used to get, but the flavor is both richer and more delicate in aroma.

1 (3.75-ounce) can oil-packed sardines, drained

2 tablespoons mayonnaise

1 teaspoon hot sauce

Kosher salt and freshly ground black pepper

4 slices white bread, toasted

1. In a medium bowl, gently mix the sardines with the mayonnaise and hot sauce, making sure not to break up the sardines too much. Taste and season with salt and pepper.

2. Divide the sardine mixture between 2 slices of the toast, spreading it evenly. Top each with the remaining toast to form 2 sandwiches and serve immediately.

FISH CAKES

SERVES 4

This is a recipe that can be very forgiving. The salt cod is certainly a throwback to the days when it was inexpensive and could be kept without refrigeration. Atlantic mariners had used salt cod on board ships for just those reasons and the fish had been used as a part of the diet on slave ships, in that way entering the diets of many of African descent throughout the hemisphere.

For families such as Abigail's and my own, cakes and croquettes were a 1950s way of stretching food; the proportion of fish to potato increased with the amount of money that one had. Wealthy people with more fish than potato put tartar sauce on theirs; we put ketchup on ours because they were more potato than fish. The crunch of the outside of the shallow-fried fish cake contrasts with the soft potato and meaty-chewy bits of salt cod. How savory they are depends on how long you soak the salt cod; some people prefer them soaked long enough to remove all the salt (in which case you will need to slightly salt the potato mixture), and others prefer a shorter soak to leave the salinity and flavor in the fish.

1 pound salt cod, soaked in water for 8 to 12 hours (see Notes)

1½ pounds russet potatoes, cut into ½-inch cubes

½ cup plus 1 tablespoon vegetable oil

1 large onion, minced

Kosher salt

2 tablespoons unsalted butter, at room temperature

1 large egg

1½ teaspoons freshly ground black pepper

Chopped fresh parsley, for garnish

Ketchup and/or tartar sauce, for serving (optional)

1. In a medium pot, combine the soaked cod (see Notes) and potatoes with enough water to cover them by 2 inches. Bring to a boil over high heat. Reduce to a simmer and cook until just tender, 15 to 20 minutes. Drain in a colander to cool.

2. Rinse the cod, then pat it dry with a clean kitchen towel. Remove any skin and bones from the fish, breaking up the meat into ½-inch pieces and adding it to a bowl.

3. In a cast-iron skillet, heat 1 tablespoon of the oil over medium-high heat until it shimmers. Add the onion and cook until browned on the edges but not yet translucent, 3 to 5 minutes. Season with salt and transfer to the bowl with the cod.

4. Add the cooled potatoes and butter to the bowl and mash with a fork. Season with salt. Add the egg and black pepper, mixing until combined. Divide the mixture into 4 equal portions and shape them into cakes 4 inches across and about 1 inch thick.

5. Line a plate with paper towels and have nearby. In the same cast-iron skillet, heat the remaining ½ cup oil over medium-high heat until it shimmers. Working in batches if necessary, add the cakes to the pan and cook until golden brown on both sides, about 3 minutes per side. Drain briefly on the paper towels.

6. Garnish with the parsley. Serve with ketchup and/or tartar sauce.

NOTES: Soak the cod in at least 2 quarts of water, in the refrigerator, for 8 to 12 hours. Change the water after a few hours to remove salt more quickly.

If the soaked cod is tender enough to break apart without cooking, you can skip cooking the cod and just go to the step where you add it to a bowl.

B&M BAKED BEANS

SERVES 6 TO 8

An old adage defines Massachusetts as "the home of the bean and the cod." The state is certainly the home of the baked bean: a dish whose Native American origins cannot be disputed. Abigail's Northern family does not disappoint with a recipe, in the traditional form of a sweet bake dotted with salty bits. She, like a true Yankee, calls for B&M baked beans—a regional brand—noting that they, unlike other more prevalent and popular brands do not contain tomatoes and are prepared with molasses, a reminder of the Northern Colonial connections to the cane-growing Caribbean. Abigail's dish follows the African American dictate of "doctoring up" something by fiddling with and adding one's own personal fillips—in Abigail's case, the orange juice. Accompanied by store-bought B&M canned brown bread, this is a part of the regional fare craved by Black Yankees.

1 (28-ounce) can B&M Original Baked Beans

¼ cup (packed) dark brown sugar

1 cup freshly squeezed orange juice, water, or pineapple juice

8 ounces salt pork, cut into ½-inch cubes and fried crisp (optional)

1 cup canned crispy fried onions

1. Preheat the oven to 350°F.

2. In a 9 × 13-inch baking dish, mix together the baked beans, brown sugar, and orange juice. Place the salt pork (if using) in the center of the dish. Cover tightly with aluminum foil.

3. Bake for 20 minutes. Uncover, top with the fried onions, and bake until the beans are bubbling hot and the top is slightly browned and caramelized, about 10 more minutes.

4. Serve hot.

CORN PUDDING

SERVES 6 TO 8

Another New England classic was often on the table for Abigail, but this time with the twist of using a corn bread mix as a base for the pudding. The use of a prepackaged mix was just fine in many households, as long as taste wasn't sacrificed, and as many old-fashioned brands of corn bread mix simply contain the premeasured and seasoned dry ingredients (flour, baking powder, etc.) it saves the measuring time.

Abigail's family included her Harlem Renaissance poet mother and her aunt, writer Dorothy West, and she noted that, "Labor-saving was an issue in the household with working women who were also writers and trying to find and make time for themselves to create." This recipe fits right in with the African American idea of "doctorin' it up" (as did her baked bean recipe on page 182). Certainly, the notion of putting your own twist on something standard is not exclusive, but for many African American families, accustomed to personal histories of migration and therefore adaptation to new places, cultures, communities, and yes, foods, modifying recipes and products is also a way of adapting to time and place.

In this case, the corn bread mix is fixed with both creamed and whole corn kernels as well as whipped egg whites, to give the pudding a rich, sweet flavor with a light texture.

2 (8.5-ounce) boxes corn muffin mix, such as Jiffy

1 (14.75-ounce) can cream-style corn

1 cup corn kernels, fresh, thawed, or canned

⅓ cup sugar

¼ cup heavy cream, or ½ cup whole milk

1 teaspoon kosher salt

¼ teaspoon freshly ground black pepper

4 large eggs, separated

1. Preheat the oven to 400°F. Spray a 9 × 13-inch baking dish with cooking spray.

2. In a large bowl, stir together the corn muffin mix, cream-style corn, corn kernels, sugar, heavy cream, salt, and pepper until well combined. Whisk the yolks into the batter.

3. In a separate clean bowl, beat the egg whites to form stiff peaks, 4 to 5 minutes.

4. Using a spatula, gently fold half the egg whites into the cornmeal batter until just combined, then fold in the remaining egg whites. Pour the batter into the baking dish.

5. Bake until the edges of the pudding are lightly browned and the top is slightly puffed, 40 to 50 minutes.

6. Let cool in the pan on a wire rack for 10 minutes. Serve warm.

PINKSTER DAY AND JONKONNU

While most Americans now know of Juneteenth (see page 207), the newest federal holiday, few who do not live in the upstate New York area have heard of Pinkster Day. And few who don't live in coastal North Carolina have heard of Jonkonnu or Johnkannaus. Both are early African American holidays first celebrated during the period of enslavement that speak to the multiplicity of African American experiences.

Pinkster Day is celebrated on Pentecost or Whitsuntide, which occurs fifty days after Easter. For the seventeenth-century Dutch, secular festivities associated with Pinkster transformed it into a spring festival. It was a time for baptisms, churchgoing, and a break from work. There were also Pinkster markets, at which the enslaved (yes, people of African descent were enslaved in New York at the time) sold goods; the profits from which they used for their celebrations.

Over the years, Pinkster developed an African American component. The Sunday was a religious holiday for all including the enslaved, but on Monday, and for between three to five days following, the enslaved were given passes that enabled them to travel and reunite with family and friends. By the nineteenth century, Pinkster had become an African American festival complete with drumming and dancing and was celebrated as such. It almost died out, but was retained in memory and in more recent times has been reestablished in some communities.

Today, Historic Hudson Valley re-creates Pinkster at Philipsburg Manor in Sleepy Hollow, New York. In 2024, there was even a Pinkster stroll from the Dyckman Farmhouse in northern Manhattan to the New-York Historical Society on the West Side designed to raise awareness of the African American holiday.

Jonkonnu, Johnkannaus, Jankonnu, Junkonoo, or John Canoe are some of the ways that *this* holiday has been spelled in the historic record. Harriet Jacobs, who was enslaved in North Carolina, described the holiday in *Incidents in the Life of a Slave Girl* as "bands of slaves masquerading in rags playing music on a 'gumbo box.'" In an African parallel to the European caroling, the enslaved would go from plantation to plantation requesting or demanding Christmas donations, which they received in the form of money or liquor. The practice relates to similar ones in Jamaica and the Bahamas, with variations of the same name, and was revived in the twenty-first century by Tryon Palace, a replica of the 1770s British Royal Governor's mansion located in New Bern, North Carolina. The events seem to commemorate an eighteenth-century Akan warrior—possibly named John Canoe or John Conny or January Conny—who fought against European traders.

Both Pinkster and Jonkonnu are testaments to the ability to create pockets of joy amidst unspeakable situations, and especially to the enduring survival of African cultures in the United States.

CULINARY CREATIVE

CHARLOTTE LYONS

I met Charlotte Lyons at a market-research event organized by a food brand in a wintery-cold Midwestern city. The company had assembled a group of African American chefs and food writers to discuss potential new products. I remember recipe testing, the immaculate test kitchens, and the jokes shared about how African Americans liked their desserts incredibly sweet—sweeter than the lovely Midwestern ladies of the test kitchen had ever made anything. I remember the conviviality and laughter and sitting up after the meetings in the hotel bar to chat and talk about our worlds. It was the beginning of what is now a multidecade friendship.

Charlotte was then just starting her career at *Ebony* magazine, where she was the food editor for more than twenty-five years, and I was then teaching full time at Queens College while pursuing my work with the food, foodways, and culture of the African diaspora as a tangential hobby. From the beginning, though, Charlotte and I bonded over many things, not the least of which was that we were some of the very few African Americans working in the realm of food media back then. If I journeyed to Chicago, I'd spend time with her in her office in the now-iconic test kitchen in the Johnson Publishing headquarters, known to all as the *Ebony* Building.

The *Ebony* Building was a Chicago landmark and a totem for many Black Americans. *Ebony* magazine had been on the coffee table at my house for as far back as I could remember. *Ebony*, with its view of the world on the Black side, gave us all a counterbalance and corrective to the negative news and pictures that were usually seen. Movie stars were profiled in their homes; business, professional, and religious leaders were shown with families; and Blackness and Black excellence were celebrated. For that alone (but there was so much more), the magazine was a source of great pride and on the coffee tables of many African American homes in midcentury America.

John Johnson, *Ebony*'s founder, understood the weight that the magazine had in the African American world, and the corporate headquarters on Chicago's South Side lived up to the aspirations expressed in the magazine . . . and to the world that lived between its pages. It was a hymn to possibility wrought in wood and stone. Up to date in every way, it expressed the desires of African Americans and Johnson's attainment of the promise expressed in the American Dream, and nowhere in the building more so than in the Day-Glo orange test kitchen in which Charlotte worked daily.

Within those walls, Charlotte not only worked with the traditional recipes that she'd been taught as a child in Atlanta, but she also rang in changes that modernized the classics, connected people with the foods of the African diaspora, and generally demonstrated the innovative ways that African Americans have long had with our country's food.

Charlotte was well prepared for it. Her love of food grew from the times she spent with family growing up in Atlanta, where the family's fresh vegetables were grown by her grandfather, on a plot of land given to him at the bus depot where he worked. The garden also offered a locus for family communion. Her family came together across generations to prepare the food for canning and to share meals. Charlotte's involvement with cooking began at an early age. She remembers:

> My grandmother used to keep me while my mother worked, because my father was in the military over in Germany. My grandfather built a little wooden box, so I could stand on top of it and stir food because I was too small. I used to love to be in the kitchen with my grandmother. I started cooking around age six or seven. At the end of the summer, my grandmother would start her canning—her tomatoes and green beans and chowchow for the winter. So, everybody would come to her home and we would sit on her porch, and you'd either shell peas or prepare green beans or do whatever had to be done. It turned out to be very good preparation for working at Johnson Publishing.

Charlotte had other preparation as well; she'd worked in corporate food test kitchens at Betty Crocker and at Campbell's Soup.

> My degree was a Bachelor of Science in home economics, and a lot of my training was in the test kitchens, so I wasn't sure that I'd be hired for a job at a magazine as a food editor. When I went for my interview at Ebony with Mr. Johnson, he said, "Ms. Lyons, no doubt, you're qualified." I replied, "But Mr. Johnson, I'm not a journalist." And he explained what they wanted was to get really good recipes that worked for home cooks and added that he knew that with my test kitchen background I'd be able to provide those. So, I worked really hard changing some of the traditional African American recipes, making them a little lighter, a little healthier, without losing some of the flavors, because African Americans, we like a lot of flavor.

Over the years, Lyons became expert at adapting and lightening the flavors of traditional African American fare, and at keeping a finger on the pulse of changing African American culinary habits.

The culinary influence of *Ebony* magazine is incalculable. As the magazine was, for much of the second half of the twentieth century, the go-to magazine for Black Americans, its pages both reflected and influenced how we ate and how we aspired to eat. Charlotte has watched over it for twenty-five plus years, as the more classically African American dishes of the magazine's earlier years have been lightened, as current trends have taken us from eating meat-heavy dishes to being more plant-forward in our diets, and as a desire to eat more dishes from around the African diaspora has grown. She's overseen photo shoots, prepped the food, and curated the menus. She even oversaw the rewriting of *The Ebony Cookbook*.

The recipes she's shared for this chapter showcase her ability to transform classics into dishes that have more contemporary techniques and flavors. Some of these recipes are lightened or infused with techniques, ideas, and ingredients from around the globe, but all show the twin strains of adherence to the past and innovation, as witnessed by a constant search for new flavors that have traditionally been the hallmark of Black cooking.

ROASTED GOLDEN BEET SALAD

SERVES 4

In my childhood, beets were one color . . . red. They showed up in the pickled beets (see page 190) that were often on our table, and once a year as Harvard beets at Thanksgiving. And more often than not, they were canned.

Today, there is an array of hues, striated and multicolored, and readily available, as this humble vegetable achieved "star" status. Golden beets, when roasted, take on a sweetness that transforms into something that is festive and colorful. Their full flavor matches beautifully with bright, sweet citrus in the dressing. Spicy, bitter greens, like arugula, and pungent, salty cheese make this salad a beautiful mix of tastes and textures.

1 pound golden beets, scrubbed well, trimmed, and halved

3 tablespoons olive oil, plus more as needed

Kosher salt

1 teaspoon finely grated orange zest

3 tablespoons freshly squeezed orange juice

1 tablespoon fresh lemon juice

1 tablespoon minced shallot or sweet onion

½ teaspoon Dijon mustard

5 cups arugula or other mixed greens (about 5 ounces)

⅓ cup crumbled goat or feta cheese

¼ cup thinly sliced red or sweet white onion

1. Preheat the oven to 400°F. Line a sheet pan with parchment paper or aluminum foil.

2. Rub the cut sides of the beets with a little oil and place cut-sides down on the prepared pan. Roast until the beets can easily be pierced with a sharp knife, about 45 minutes.

3. Let cool enough to handle, peel the beets and discard the skins. Cut them into ½-inch cubes, place in a large serving bowl, and season with a few pinches of salt.

4. In a separate bowl, whisk together the orange zest, orange juice, lemon juice, shallot, and mustard. Whisk in the 3 tablespoons olive oil until emulsified and season with salt to taste.

5. Arrange the arugula, beets, cheese, and onion on four individual salad plates. Drizzle each with dressing and serve.

PICKLED BEETS

SERVES 4 TO 8

Charlotte's recipe is very similar to the one that was a classic on my mother's table, and can be prepared from fresh or canned beets without losing integrity. Canned beets were a pantry staple in many African American kitchens, and for many African American home cooks this was a salad or side dish that could be had at any time of the year and without the cooking time. The sweet-tart brine and hint of floral cloves go perfectly with the earthy flavor of beets.

1 pound medium beets, scrubbed well and trimmed

½ cup distilled white vinegar

¼ cup sugar

½ teaspoon kosher salt

⅛ teaspoon ground cloves

½ small white onion, thinly sliced

1. In a large saucepan, combine the beets with enough water to cover by 1 or 2 inches. Bring to a boil over high heat. Reduce the heat to medium-low and simmer until fork-tender, 25 to 30 minutes. Drain and cool.

2. In a separate glass or ceramic bowl, whisk together the vinegar, sugar, salt, and cloves until the sugar and salt dissolve.

3. Peel and cut the beets into ¼-inch-thick slices. Add them and the onions to the bowl with the vinegar mixture. Toss gently to coat.

4. Cover the bowl with plastic wrap and refrigerate at least 4 hours before serving.

SOUTHERN FRIED CORN

SERVES 6

Fresh summer-ripe corn cut off the cob, rich salt pork or smoky bacon, and butter . . . what more needs to be said? This is a Southern summer classic, though the name is a bit of a misnomer. Certainly not deep-fried, Southern fried corn is more of a saucy sauté of kernels, similar to creamed corn.

Please remember that once you've tasted corn that has been recently picked, such as ears from summer farm stands or farmers' markets, your taste profile for corn will be forever changed. There will be no going back; the fresh-from-the-stalk sweetness is that memorable.

¼ pound salt pork or slab bacon, sliced into ¼-inch-thick slices

¼ cup all-purpose flour

2 teaspoons sugar

4 cups fresh corn kernels (from 6 to 8 ears of corn)

1 tablespoon salted butter

Kosher salt

Freshly ground white pepper

1. In a large heavy skillet, cook the salt pork slices over medium heat until golden brown, 5 to 7 minutes.

2. Meanwhile, in a bowl, stir together the flour, sugar, and ¼ cup water. Add the corn and stir to form a smooth mixture with the corn kernels evenly distributed throughout.

3. Add the corn mixture and butter to the skillet. Season with salt and white pepper to taste. Increase the heat to medium-high and bring to a boil. Reduce the heat to low and simmer, stirring often to prevent sticking, until the corn is creamy, 35 to 40 minutes.

4. Serve hot.

GREENS

There are many different types of leafy greens that are used to replace the greens traditionally used in Western Africa. Most notably in the United States it's collard greens. Many are taken aback when told that collards are not in fact African greens, but rather a northern European vegetable. "Collard" is a corruption of colewort and that term refers to any non-heading cabbage. Collards were the northern European greens that were available to the enslaved, and they became used in Southern cooking to replace unavailable African greens, such as bitterleaf and cassava leaves. The Africanism in the treatment of these greens is to cook them with a piece of some form of smoked protein for seasoning, stew them long, low, and slow—until, as someone once wrote to me, "they could wink back at you." The other key aspect of the dish is the consumption of the pot likker, the vitamin-rich liquid in which the greens were cooked.

While collards are one of the most popular of the leafy greens that are consumed by African Americans, we also eat mustard greens, turnip greens, and kale, among others. Each type has its partisans. I fall firmly into the collards camp, loving their slightly metallic taste, especially when they are topped with minced onion and a dash or two of hot sauce. Maya Angelou was a fan of kale, which she served at her legendary New Year's Day parties to bring good luck and folding money, as the tradition goes.

There are other methods of cooking greens that are being more widely adopted, such as of stir-frying them in a bit of oil with garlic or simply braising them as Charlotte Lyons does (see page 193).

CAJUN-STYLE BRAISED COLLARD GREENS

SERVES 4 TO 6

Long, low, and slow cooked greens are one of the mainstays of the Southern African American table. Here, they're given an update, cut as the French would say *en chiffonade*, and braised with cayenne pepper in a tomato-y broth.

This update is interesting because it starts the greens in the traditional manner—boiled in a large pot of water—and then discards that liquid before it can become the pot likker that is so prized by lovers of traditional greens. Instead, the greens are then simmered in a small amount of broth, resulting in a more intensely flavored liquid, with the natural bitterness of the greens attenuated.

2 pounds collard greens, rinsed and drained, tough stems removed

2 teaspoons kosher salt, plus more to taste

2 tablespoons olive oil

1 medium onion, thinly sliced

5 garlic cloves, minced

½ teaspoon red pepper flakes

1 cup vegetable or chicken broth

1 large tomato, coarsely chopped

2 teaspoons dark brown sugar (optional)

1 teaspoon hot sauce

Pinch of cayenne pepper

1. Stack the collards a few at a time and roll into tight bundles. Cut each bundle crosswise into ¼-inch-wide ribbons.

2. Bring a large pot of water to a boil over high heat.

3. Add the 2 teaspoons salt and the collards, cover, reduce the heat to medium, and cook, stirring often, until the greens are barely tender, about 20 minutes. Drain well.

4. In the same pot, heat the olive oil, onion, garlic, and pepper flakes over medium-high heat and cook, stirring frequently, until the onion is translucent, about 5 minutes.

5. Add the drained collards and the broth, cover, and cook over medium heat, stirring occasionally, until tender, 8 to 10 minutes.

6. Add the tomato, brown sugar (if using), hot sauce, and cayenne. Season well with salt. Cook, covered, until the tomato has collapsed and the greens are quite tender, about 10 minutes.

7. Serve hot.

SAUTÉED GARLIC BEANS
WITH BLACK SESAME SEEDS

SERVES 2 TO 4

String beans, cooked slow like greens until meltingly tender, are a Southern staple, usually flavored with a piece of seasoning pork. They're delicious, but it's useful to remember how that dish came to be. Among other factors, old varieties of string beans could be tough and required long cooking to tenderize. Fuel was a limited resource, so cooking methods had to take full advantage of a wood fire's different stages; setting a pot to slow-cook over the warm embers was a way of maximizing use of the heat.

This recipe takes advantage of contemporary, tender varieties of green beans, using the especially young tender ones that are marketed under the French name *haricots verts*. Sautéed instead of stewed, and seasoned with garlic and Chinese flavors of sweet-savory hoisin sauce and black sesame, it pays homage to the garden-fresh summer vegetables of Charlotte's youth with a global outlook.

1. In a 12-inch nonstick skillet, heat the oil over medium heat until shimmering. Add the onion and a pinch of salt and cook until softened, 3 to 5 minutes. Stir in the garlic and the pepper flakes and cook for 20 seconds, until aromatic but not browned.

2. Increase the heat to high. Add the haricots verts, black pepper, and a pinch of salt. Cook, stirring often, until the green beans are tender but still bright green, 5 to 7 minutes.

3. Stir in the hoisin sauce until the green beans are completely coated. Taste and adjust the seasoning with more salt, pepper, or hoisin, as needed.

4. Transfer to a serving dish, sprinkle with the black sesame seeds, and serve.

2 tablespoons vegetable oil

½ small sweet onion, small diced

Kosher salt

4 to 5 garlic cloves, chopped

⅛ teaspoon red pepper flakes, or to taste

1 pound haricots verts or green beans

¼ teaspoon freshly ground black pepper, plus more to taste

2 tablespoons hoisin sauce, plus more to taste

1 tablespoon black sesame seeds

SOUTHERN FRIED CATFISH

SERVES 6

Because catfish are bottom feeders and could be muddy tasting, they were eschewed in favor of other fish by many in the South. They became one of the foods left for folks with less money. Today, however, the tasty fish are farmed, have lost their strong taste, and now turn up on tables throughout the South.

Frying in deep oil is one of the culinary techniques cited by anthropologist William Bascom as a signature of many West African cuisines. Indeed, a mastery of this form of cooking is evidenced in the number of deep-fried dishes, both savory and sweet, that are a part of the African American culinary repertoire. When this is demonstrated by delicately fried catfish, the results are a delicacy enjoyed by all and especially tasty when paired with a salad of summer fresh tomatoes like Leni's High Summer Tomato Salad (page 168).

1. Line a sheet pan with paper towels and set a wire rack (if you have one) in the pan. Place this near your stovetop.

2. Pat the catfish dry with paper towels. Arrange the fillets in a shallow dish and season well with salt and pepper. In a large shallow baking dish or in a large brown paper bag, combine the cornmeal, flour, paprika, ½ teaspoon salt, and ½ teaspoon pepper.

3. In a large heavy skillet or Dutch oven, pour 1 to 1½ inches oil into the pan (making sure there is at least 1 inch of clearance). Heat the oil over medium-high heat to 350°F.

4. Add 3 of the fillets at a time to the baking dish or paper bag and dredge or shake to coat.

5. Add the 3 fillets to the hot oil and fry until golden brown on both sides, 3 to 4 minutes per side. Transfer to the paper towels (or the rack) to drain. Repeat with the next batch and serve hot.

6 skin-on catfish fillets (6 ounces each)

Kosher salt and freshly ground black pepper

1½ cups stone-ground yellow cornmeal

½ cup all-purpose flour

⅛ teaspoon sweet paprika

6 cups vegetable oil, for frying

BROILED CATFISH TACOS
WITH CHIPOTLE SAUCE

SERVES 6

One of the ways that the traditional fried catfish might turn up on the modern table is as the main ingredient in catfish tacos. Of course, you could take the crisp-fried cornmeal-crusted catfish from page 197 and serve them in tortillas with the spicy-smoky rich chipotle sauce.

This version is a lighter, though no less flavorful, spin on the traditional fried fish. The recipe calls for marinating the catfish fillets and then broiling them for a spicy, brighter taste.

1 teaspoon chili powder

½ teaspoon ground cumin

¼ teaspoon garlic powder

Kosher salt

2 tablespoons olive oil

1 pound skinned catfish fillets, ½ inch thick, skin off, patted dry

6 (6-inch) corn tortillas or hard taco shells

Juice of 1 lime

Chopped fresh cilantro

FOR SERVING

Chipotle Sauce (recipe follows)

Chopped tomato

Diced avocado

Shredded lettuce or cabbage

Crumbled cotija cheese

1. In a bowl, stir together the chili powder, cumin, garlic powder, a few generous pinches of salt, and the oil. Add the fish and gently toss to coat. Let stand for about 15 minutes.

2. Position an oven rack close to the broiler element and turn the broiler on high.

3. On a broiler pan, arrange the fish in a single layer and broil until the fish flakes easily with a fork, 4 to 6 minutes, flipping it halfway through.

4. Meanwhile, lay the tortillas or hard taco shells out in one layer on a baking sheet. When the fish comes out of the oven, immediately place the tortillas under the broiler or heat the taco shells according to the package instructions.

5. Transfer the cooked fish to a platter, drizzle with the lime juice, and scatter the chopped cilantro over the top. Take the tortillas out of the oven and stack to preserve warmth.

6. **TO SERVE:** Fill the tortillas or hard taco shells with the catfish mixture and serve immediately with the chipotle sauce, chopped tomato, diced avocado, shredded lettuce or cabbage, and crumbled cotija cheese.

CHIPOTLE SAUCE
MAKES ABOUT ½ CUP

This spicy and creamy sauce is great as an accompaniment to the tacos, but works equally well with fried fish or drizzled onto roasted or fried chicken.

⅓ cup mayonnaise

1 tablespoon sour cream or buttermilk

1 or 2 minced canned chipotle peppers in adobo sauce, to taste

2 tablespoons minced fresh cilantro

1. In a small bowl, stir together the mayonnaise, sour cream, chipotles, and cilantro. Store in an airtight container in the refrigerator until ready to use.

KOOL-AID PUNCH

MAKES ABOUT ½ GALLON

Laugh if you must, but Kool-Aid was the champagne on many an African American dinner table for decades. Doctored up with other ingredients, it provided color, fun, and something out of the ordinary instead of water at many meals. In my family, my paternal grandmother, Ida Irene Harris, prepared her grape Kool-Aid with cut-up lemons and I remember it as my childhood elixir of the gods. Other African Americans across many age groups have similar memories, so much so that Philadelphia chef Omar Tate has created his own proprietary mix in honor of the Kool-Aid of his childhood.

Here, Charlotte uses Kool-Aid in a punch recipe similar to those that might have appeared in the pages of *Ebony* magazine in the 1950s. (For the photo, see the drink on page 204.)

3 cups hot water

2 cups sugar

2 (0.16-ounce) packets Kool-Aid, any flavor

1 (14-ounce) can crushed pineapple, undrained

⅓ cup maraschino cherries, with their juices

1 liter ginger ale, chilled

1. In a large pitcher, mix together the hot water and sugar, stirring until the sugar has dissolved. Add the powdered Kool-Aid, pineapple, and maraschino cherries, stirring until combined.

2. Refrigerate for 2 to 3 hours, until well chilled. Add the ginger ale just before serving.

FAMILY REUNIONS

Family reunions, as a concept, certainly belong to no one community. But they—and the term—hold special import in African American culture.

Some people feel that family reunions for African Americans date back to the years of the Great Migration, when families wanted to stay in touch with members who had moved North or West. I contend that things start a little earlier, and in fact probably go back to the days following Emancipation. One of the startling things that occurred then is that African American newspapers around the country were filled with ads placed by the formerly enslaved trying to find and reconnect with family members from whom they had been separated. Because for centuries so many families had been brutally broken up and scattered, family is precious to African Americans. It is as simple as that. No matter how crazy they make you, they're yours. Contemporary family reunions are joyful gatherings with differences put aside.

Summertime is now the classic season for Black family reunions, perhaps because it is when most vacations are taken and when children are out of school. Family reunions are no small thing for African Americans. Gatherings may include as many as four hundred people. Nowadays you can spot them at the airports, boarding trains, or heading up the cruise ship gangplank in matching T-shirts all proclaiming membership in whatever family is being celebrated.

Once at the venue, it's all about basking in the warmth of family and eating—food taking a very special spot at most reunions, from the arguments about who makes the best potato salad (and whose to avoid at all costs), to whose cake is the year's best and which ones are always the first to go. It's a time for some gentle family competition and a joyous time for all. Having family around to cherish was not always possible and so today's family reunions are a large part of the Black Joy of the contemporary African American experience.

OLD-FASHIONED SWEET POTATO CAKE

SERVES 12 TO 16

This old-fashioned sweet potato cake is a recipe that Charlotte's great-grandmother, coincidentally named Jessie Harris (or "Ma Jessie" to the family—and no relation of mine), used to prepare for family gatherings.

Each generation of Charlotte's family had a stellar baker who had a signature cake. Ma Jessie's developed when they had a bumper crop of sweet potatoes on her farm in Stockbridge, Georgia, but the prize recipe came to be reserved for holidays and special occasions.

The ubiquity of sweet potatoes in the traditional Southern African American diet is spoken to by their turning up on Leni Sorensen's table as well (see Oven-Baked Yams, page 162). Often, they provided the only taste of sweetness in a meal.

This cake is tender and moist from the sweet potatoes and studded with nuts and coconut for richness. It's a delightful surprise on any Southern dessert table. (For the photo, see the bottom left of page 204.)

CAKE

Softened unsalted butter and flour, for the pan

16 tablespoons (2 sticks) unsalted butter, at room temperature

2 cups granulated sugar

2½ cups cooked mashed sweet potatoes (see Note)

4 large eggs, at room temperature

1¼ teaspoons vanilla extract

3 cups all-purpose flour

2 teaspoons baking powder

1 teaspoon baking soda

1 teaspoon ground cinnamon

½ teaspoon freshly grated nutmeg

¼ teaspoon kosher salt

½ cup chopped walnuts or pecans

½ cup unsweetened flaked coconut

ICING

2 cups powdered sugar, sifted

1 teaspoon finely grated orange zest

1 teaspoon finely grated lemon zest

3 tablespoons fresh lemon juice

1. **MAKE THE CAKE:** Preheat the oven to 350°F. Butter and flour a 10-inch tube pan.

2. In a stand mixer fitted with the paddle (or in a bowl with a hand mixer), beat the butter and granulated sugar on medium speed for about 3 minutes, until light and fluffy. Stop to scrape down the bowl. Add the sweet potatoes and beat on medium-low speed for about 2 minutes, until thoroughly combined. Add the eggs, one at a time, beating well after each addition. Beat in the vanilla.

3. In a large bowl, whisk together the flour, baking powder, baking soda, cinnamon, nutmeg, and salt. On low speed, gradually add the flour mixture to the sweet potato mixture, beating just until just combined.

4. By hand, fold in the walnuts and coconut until evenly distributed. Pour the batter into the pan, spreading it evenly.

5. Bake until a tester inserted into the cake comes out clean, about 1 hour 15 minutes.

6. Let the cake cool in the pan on a wire rack for about 5 minutes. Then invert the cake onto the rack.

7. **WHILE THE CAKE IS STILL HOT, MAKE THE ICING:** In a medium bowl, whisk together the powdered sugar, orange zest, lemon zest, and lemon juice until smooth. Spread the icing evenly over the warm cake.

8. Cool completely before serving.

NOTE: Cook about 4 medium sweet potatoes according to the method in Oven-Baked Yams (page 162). When cool enough to handle, peel, mash, and measure the 2½ cups you need here.

BROWN SUGAR POUND CAKE

SERVES 12 TO 16

In matters of desserts, the African American palate remains one that *loves* sweet desserts. This is a brown sugar pound cake that has lasted the test of time in Charlotte's family, with few changes. A generation after Ma Jessie Harris's (*not* me!) sweet potato cake recipe entered into the family repertoire, this cake was developed by Ma Jessie's daughter—Charlotte's great-aunt, Myra Harris Slaughter. Here Charlotte has lightened it up while retaining the classic pound cake taste. With the light molasses flavor of brown sugar both in the cake and in the glaze, and a generous helping of nuts and coconut, this has a depth that sets it apart from other pound cakes. (For a photo, see the top right of the opposite page.)

CAKE

Softened unsalted butter and cake flour, for the pan

3⅓ cups cake flour, sifted

½ teaspoon baking powder

1 teaspoon kosher salt

1 cup vegetable shortening, at room temperature

8 tablespoons (1 stick) unsalted butter, at room temperature

1 pound light brown sugar

1 cup granulated sugar

5 large eggs, at room temperature

1½ teaspoons vanilla extract

1 cup evaporated milk

1 cup unsweetened flaked coconut

1 cup chopped walnuts or pecans

GLAZE

About 5 tablespoons (⅓ cup) unsalted butter

1 cup (packed) light brown sugar

¼ cup evaporated milk

1 teaspoon vanilla extract

1. MAKE THE CAKE: Preheat the oven to 325°F. Butter and flour a 10-inch tube pan.

2. In a medium bowl, whisk together the flour, baking powder, and salt.

3. In a stand mixer fitted with the paddle, beat the shortening and butter on medium-high speed for about 2 minutes, until combined. Add both of the sugars and beat on medium-high speed for about 3 minutes, until light and fluffy. Stop to scrape down the bowl.

4. Reduce the speed to medium-low and add the eggs, one at a time, beating well after each addition. Beat in the vanilla.

5. Alternating with the evaporated milk, add the flour mixture in several additions, beating to form a smooth batter. Using a spatula, fold in the coconut and walnuts. Distribute the batter evenly into the pan, smoothing the surface.

6. Bake until a tester inserted in the cake comes out clean, about 1 hour 40 minutes.

7. Let the cake cool in the pan on a wire rack set over a baking sheet for 10 minutes. Carefully invert the cake from the pan onto the rack to cool completely.

8. MEANWHILE, MAKE THE GLAZE: In a medium saucepan, melt the butter and brown sugar over medium heat, stirring until the sugar has dissolved. Stir in the evaporated milk, increase the heat to medium-high, bring to a boil, and cook until thick but spreadable, 2 to 3 minutes. Remove from the heat and stir in the vanilla.

9. Spread the glaze over the cooled cake and serve.

PEACH BREAD PUDDING CUPCAKES
WITH BOURBON GLAZE

MAKES 24 CUPCAKES

Bread puddings were a way for thrifty cooks to make use of stale bread. It's a dessert particularly beloved in New Orleans, and Creole chefs have created myriad variations.

This contemporary version of the recipe forms the pudding into cupcake-like individual servings that surprise with a kick of bourbon glaze, and a sweet-tart fillip of peaches to give all that richness a balance. If there is any leftover bourbon glaze, don't discard it . . . try drizzling it over ice cream!

CUPCAKES

1 cup frozen sliced peaches, thawed slightly (or fresh if in season) and cut into 1-inch cubes

⅓ cup bourbon

7 cups (loosely packed) bite-sized cubes day-old French bread (about 1 baguette)

½ cup chopped pecans

1¼ cups whole milk

1¼ cups half-and-half

1 cup granulated sugar

3 large eggs, at room temperature

4 tablespoons (½ stick) unsalted butter, melted and slightly cooled

1 tablespoon vanilla extract

½ teaspoon freshly grated nutmeg

¼ teaspoon ground cinnamon

¼ teaspoon kosher salt

GLAZE

4 tablespoons (½ stick) unsalted butter

¾ cup powdered sugar

1 tablespoon bourbon

⅛ teaspoon kosher salt

1. MAKE THE CUPCAKES: In a small bowl, mix together the peaches and bourbon and let macerate for 15 minutes.

2. Position oven racks in the upper and lower thirds of the oven and preheat to 350°F. Line the cups of two standard muffin tins with paper liners and grease with cooking spray.

3. In a large bowl, add the bread cubes and scatter the pecans over them. Pour the peaches and their juices over the bread.

4. In a medium bowl, whisk together the milk, half-and-half, granulated sugar, eggs, melted butter, vanilla, nutmeg, cinnamon, and salt until well blended. Pour the mixture over the peaches and stir gently until the bread is coated. Let the mixture sit for 15 minutes. Gently stir again to ensure everything is evenly incorporated.

5. Using an ice cream scoop or ⅓-cup measuring cup, fill the muffin cups two-thirds of the way with bread mixture.

6. Bake on the upper and lower racks until the pudding is slightly puffed and golden brown, about 45 minutes, switching racks and rotating the muffin tins front to back halfway through.

7. Remove the cupcakes from the muffin tin and transfer to a wire rack set in a sheet pan to cool.

8. MAKE THE GLAZE: In a small saucepan, combine the butter and powdered sugar. Cook over medium heat, stirring often, until the butter and sugar melt together, about 5 minutes.

9. Remove from the heat and whisk in the bourbon and salt to form a thin glaze. Cool for about 15 minutes; it will thicken slightly. Stir until smooth and drizzle about 1 teaspoon of glaze over each cooled cupcake, reserving the rest for another use. Serve warm.

JUNETEENTH

On June 19, 1865, Major General Gordon Granger, head of the Union forces recently arrived in the port city of Galveston, Texas, and read General Order No. 3 from his headquarters.

> *The people in Texas are informed that, in accordance with a proclamation from the Executive of the United States, all slaves are free. This involves an absolute equality of personal rights and rights of property between former masters and slaves, and the connection heretofore existing between them becomes that between employer and hired labor.*
>
> *The freedmen are advised to remain quietly at their present homes and work for wages. They are informed that they will not be allowed to collect at military posts and that they will not be supported in idleness either there or elsewhere. By order of Major General Granger.*

The enslaved in Texas had remained in bondage two and a half years after Lincoln's 1863 Emancipation Proclamation had freed the enslaved in enemy territory; they must have thought that Watch Night (as they had designated the eve of Emancipation) had passed them by. The delayed proclamation must have therefore been even more riveting. Those rendered free must have been astounded by the news; reports tell of jubilation, but also of people wandering off, dumbstruck, attempting to digest it all.

By 1866, the news had been well processed, and people returned to Galveston and made pilgrimages to the spot. Many of these early Juneteenth celebrations honored those who had toiled in Texas fields. They featured prayers, parades, singing, and readings of the Proclamation. Honoring the formerly enslaved and raising up the race were the goals of the early celebrations, so much so that resistance also formed, with African Americans barred from using public property for festivities. In Houston, local ministers raised funds and purchased what became Emancipation Park so that they could have a place to celebrate.

Food and drink have always been an integral part of these celebrations. At first, the holiday feasting celebrated the abundance that came with Emancipation, with those who had been enslaved at the central tables. Early images show flower-draped carts and guests and celebrants decked out in elegant finery. The holiday grew in importance, but remained mainly a Texas thing.

By the 1950s and 1960s the Texas holiday almost fell by the wayside, only to be revived in the 1970s and '80s. Since then, it has grown in importance yearly.

Texas adopted Juneteenth as a state holiday in 1980 and several other states have followed suit. Juneteenth (also known as Emancipation Day or Freedom Day) the only nationally celebrated commemoration of the ending of slavery in the United States, became a federal holiday in 2021.

OMNIVOROUS CURATOR

JESSICA B. HARRIS

How do I begin to talk about myself? It's very difficult to define me culinarily, and perhaps culturally. I am a grandchild of the Great Migration. My early years were spent at the confluence of two very different threads of African American food. My young adulthood was spent in the company of a range of Black artists with cosmopolitan worldviews. My professional life as a college teacher and my avocation as a culinary historian have allowed me to delve deeply into the cultures and cuisines of the African Atlantic world. I have dined with a Nobel laureate and had more than one glass of rum in a beach shack with the local "bar association." I am a daughter of America and the world at large, and as such, I always look at cuisines as the confluences of place, people, and history. And that history is more often than not on the plate.

My father's elder brothers, both cooks, came North from mid-Tennessee in the 1920s. They settled, established themselves, and then sent for my grandmother and their three younger siblings, who joined them in New York around 1925. They resided in the Williamsburg section of Brooklyn, and like many of that generation of the Great Migration brought their Southern ways to New York City. I didn't know my paternal grandfather, but by the time I arrived on the scene, my paternal grandmother was firmly established in New York with her church, her relatives, and her victory garden, a plot behind the South Jamaica projects where she lived. My paternal grandmother was out of the hardscrabble South. Her Southern foodways were those of neckbones and ham hocks, of stewed mustard greens, and okra. Corn bread, made with white meal and cooked in a cast-iron skillet on the top of the stove, was Grandma Harris's go-to bread. But on special occasions there were beaten biscuits, which she whacked away at with a hammer. My father always preferred these foods, and my mother learned how to cook them for him.

My mother's family was from Roanoke, Virginia. My maternal grandmother and grandfather had met at a Virginia seminary in the late nineteenth century. When my grandfather was given the pastorate of a church in New Jersey, they moved North and my mother, the fourth of their ten children, was born in Elizabeth, New Jersey. Their Southern roots were more genteel, and one prized picture that I have of them proudly shows three generations posed on the front porch of a family house in Roanoke. My maternal grandmother's food was very different from my paternal grandmother's.

Perhaps it was that my family mainly visited on holidays, but Grandma Jones served big roasts of meat accompanied by garden vegetables with freshly baked Parker House rolls. There was always some form of preserves. I can still recall the taste of the pickled Seckel pears, and the watermelon rind pickles that would accompany the meats in the crystal relish dish that always graced the table. Both were good, in fact both were delicious, and I am a product of both sides of my family . . . with several more additions.

My personal food story becomes even more complicated when I begin to talk about my mother and some of the other foods that she placed nightly on our family table. While her roots were Southern—and out of the African American Virginia style of cooking epitomized by Edna Lewis—she was Northern raised and was a trained dietitian, a profession that very much influenced our daily eating. She had majored in dietetics at Pratt Institute in the 1930s. As a result of all this, her cooking was informed not only by the foods of her mother, her Northern upbringing, and the deep Southern ways that she learned from my paternal grandmother, but also by the ideas then prevailing in the world of dietetics about what a balanced diet was supposed to be. I grew up eating a well-composed plate with a protein (and there was always some form of animal protein!), two vegetables, and a salad made with iceberg lettuce. If we ran out of the sliced white bread that was supposed to build strong bodies twelve ways, then Mom would whip up a batch of hot bread from scratch using no measuring cup, but only her hands and a mastery of the proper look and feel of the dough. Some nights it might be Southern biscuits, others it was corn bread, prepared with only a pinch of sugar (it's not cake, she would always remind me). The American braid was on the table nightly during my mid-century childhood. In fact, as with many middle-income African American families, our nightly eating habits, while having definite African American inflections, also harked to the prevailing American norms. We ate the braid.

My culinary journey was also informed by my schooling: I spent my youth eating the world at the tables of my friends from the United Nations International School, and later added such fillips as fresh garlic and mushrooms through two years of studying in France. The American braid of the meals of my youth was extended, but the African American traditions of my childhood remained the bedrock of my food memories.

They were so deeply a part of me that while I was the travel editor at *Essence* magazine in the 1970s, I became intrigued by the similarities that I tasted between the foods I grew up with, and those that I tasted in my travels around the African diaspora. Eventually, as a cookbook author and food historian, I got to continue to travel the African Atlantic world and connect the culinary dots, taking the tastes that I'd learned at my parental table and finding them and their culinary cousins in the kitchens of the friends that I made on multiple continents. I found the taste of my mother's pig's feet in the souse of Barbados, the crispy chew of my father's favorite hard-fried *griots de porc* tasted in a restaurant called Le Rond Point in Port-au-Prince, Haiti. The more I tasted the United States versions of foods and compared them to those of other places, the more I became intrigued with the connections and the complexities of the threads that make up the braided cuisines of this country.

Gradually, over the years of eating the African diaspora and of deepening my understanding of some of the African American foodways of the South as a founding member of the Southern Foodways Alliance, and later as the owner of a home in New Orleans, I began to see the food on my table and on the tables of my friends around the country as the culmination of a conjoining of cultures.

One day, when preparing a speech, it came to me that the foundational food of the United States is a tripartite braid formed from the three cultures of the Native Americans, European Americans, and African Americans. The African American one has been the focus of my culinary life, and in many ways is a dominant one for the country because of African Americans' initial place at the bottom, working rung on the food chain of this country.

The recipes that I present here range from the traditional African American ones that I grew up with, like my mother's fried chicken and my father's hard-fried pork chops, to the iceberg lettuce salad that marked my childhood and those of many of my generation. There are cookies that I baked with my mother, as well as the tomato chutney that obsessed me for many summers. My maternal grandmother's watermelon rind pickles and her pickled peaches are here, as well as the cheat on baked ham that appeared on my New Year's buffet for many years. The recipes in this section are more numerous than other offerings from my friends, because they show the development of the American Braid and its variations in an individual household over the generations, from the pig's feet that my father taught my mother to love, through the roast chicken that is a culinary classic, ending with the apple pie that is celebrated as being the quintessential "American" dish. (We considered putting the pie on the cover of this book, until we realized that it limited the story, and in the end we opted for the table laden with Native cornmeal-crusted African okra, served with European ham.)

My meals remain grounded in my African American heritage, but are influenced by my tastes and my travels. I, like all African Americans, know that our cuisine is not monolithic and that we come from a multiplicity of culinary threads. We make and eat not only the strands of the braid that are our own complex American world, but also consume with gusto the world at large.

CLASSIC BLACK-EYED PEAS

SERVES 6

Field peas, like the black-eyed peas in this recipe, are a gift to the cooking of this hemisphere from Africa. They were brought over on slave ships and used by early African American farmers to fix nitrogen in the soil and in crop rotation. As with many traditional African American foods, they are prepared with a seasoning piece of smoked meat, but that can be switched out for smoked turkey or just left out for a different taste, one that celebrates the meatiness of the bean itself.

Which brings me to this point: This is a very simple recipe, where the quality of the individual ingredients truly matters. If simply boiling beans seems like intolerably bland food to you, try it with high-quality beans or dried peas, perhaps from small farmers or heirloom producers such as Anson Mills or Rancho Gordo. You may be stunned by the deep flavor the beans have all by themselves. Be sure to season well with salt—add a little and taste, and continue doing so until the flavor is maximized (if not the saltiness).

1 pound dried black-eyed peas

4 thick-cut slices bacon, or ¼ pound salt pork, cut into small dice

1 small onion, chopped

Kosher salt

1. Spread the beans on a baking sheet and pick through them, removing any stones, broken beans, or other debris.

2. Transfer to a heavy soup pot or large Dutch oven, add enough water to cover, and soak them overnight (at least 8 hours, until plumped). Drain in a colander and rinse well.

3. Add the diced bacon to the empty soup pot or Dutch oven. Cook over medium heat until the fat has rendered and the bacon is just beginning to brown but not crisp, about 5 minutes.

4. Add the black-eyed peas, the onion, and enough water to cover the beans by 2 inches, at least 4 cups of water.

5. Increase the heat to medium-high and bring to a boil. Reduce the heat to low, cover, and simmer until the beans are tender and the liquid has begun to thicken. The cooking time can vary with the age of the beans, so start checking at 30 minutes, but they might cook for 1 hour or more. Check every 10 minutes or so, adding warm water if necessary to keep them well submerged. (Very old beans may eventually cook through and begin to burst, but may not feel entirely smooth.) Season well with salt.

6. When the beans are nearly done, adjust the seasoning one more time; it should taste flavorful enough to be served with plain rice. Serve hot.

OLD-FASHIONED ICEBERG SALAD

SERVES 4 TO 6

It gets dolled up as a wedge and served with bacon bits and blue cheese dressing in steakhouses around the country, but for decades, in the days before arugula and mesclun, iceberg was what you got when you asked for lettuce. This is a simple salad of lettuce, tomato, cucumber, and onion that was the gold standard salad for many decades. It was the salad of my childhood. While considered the most traditional (or perhaps you might say "old-fashioned" or "boring") salad of the American braid, think for a moment of the origins of the ingredients. Tomatoes are from the New World. Cucumbers, from India. Onions are thought to be originally from Central Asia, and lettuce is believed to be from the Caucasus region. Even the most ordinary dish reveals great intermingling of histories.

1 small head iceberg lettuce, cored and thickly sliced

2 tomatoes, thickly sliced

1 red onion, thinly sliced

1 small cucumber, peeled, seeded, and cut crosswise into thin rounds

2 tablespoons cider vinegar

Pinch of sugar

Kosher salt and freshly ground black pepper

¼ cup olive oil

1. On a serving platter, mound or pile the slices of lettuce. Arrange or layer the tomatoes, onion, and cucumber over the lettuce.

2. In a small bowl, whisk together the cider vinegar and sugar. Season with salt and pepper, and slowly drizzle in the oil, whisking until well combined.

3. Spoon the dressing over the salad and serve immediately.

DEVILED EGGS

MAKES 24 DEVILED EGGS

Deviled eggs were always wrapped in waxed paper and placed in a shoebox meal that was typical of African American road trips in the days when on-the-road hospitality was not guaranteed. They're a quintessential food of the Green Book era. At the other end of the entertaining spectrum, they were also served in my home atop one of the deviled egg plates that I collect. This version is the deviled egg at its purest: The filling is simply the yolks of the eggs, whipped with mayonnaise and mustard, with the requisite dash of hot sauce. Cook the eggs just a minute or two longer than "jammy" for the creamiest filling; fully hard-boil them for a fluffier texture. They are called stuffed eggs in England.

These summer favorites can also be varied with different fillings like sweet pickle relish, salmon, or crab added to the egg mixture.

12 large eggs, hard-boiled and peeled
¼ cup mayonnaise
1 teaspoon yellow mustard
Dash of hot sauce
Kosher salt
Smoked paprika, for garnish

1. Cut each egg in half lengthwise and carefully remove the yolks without tearing the egg white halves.

2. In a bowl, mash the yolks with the mayonnaise until well combined. Stir in the mustard, and hot sauce. Taste and season with salt as needed.

3. Spoon equal amounts of the deviled yolk mixture into each egg white half. Place in a container, cover, and refrigerate for at least 1 hour, or until ready to serve.

4. Sprinkle smoked paprika on each deviled egg and serve.

ESCOVITCH

SERVES 4

I have spent more than five decades traveling and eating in the Caribbean, where Africans have left their indelibly strong mark on the culture—another place with its own version of a foundational braid of Indigenous, European, and African cultures, inflected by more than two centuries of foods from South Asian and Chinese communities. I have visited most of the countries in that region, which author Mark Kurlansky calls "a continent of islands." One of my favorite places is Jamaica, and I tell people that I am hard-core because for years I would travel to Kingston, stay with friends, visit galleries and museums, and completely eschew the beaches of the north coast. I even survived Hurricane Gilbert while visiting a friend there. That was when I learned to savor this preparation that combines a vinegary marinade with the heat of Scotch bonnet chiles, a flurry of sliced onions and bell peppers, and the delicious flakiness of freshly fried fish. Not only is the dish delicious, it also tells an interesting culinary anecdote as the name teaches that Jamaica was a colony of Spain before it was British. Then, this dish would have been called *pescado en escabeche*.

FISH

Vegetable oil, for frying

4 skin-on white fish fillets (6 to 8 ounces each), such as snapper

Kosher salt and freshly ground black pepper

MARINADE

2 medium onions, thinly sliced

2 medium carrots, scrubbed well and cut lengthwise into thin strips

1 green bell pepper, sliced into thin strips

1 Scotch bonnet or habanero chile, seeded and sliced into thin strips, or to taste

½ teaspoon black peppercorns

½ teaspoon cracked allspice berries, plus 3 whole berries

3 fresh thyme sprigs

1½ cups cane vinegar (or 1½ cups cider vinegar plus 1 tablespoon dark brown sugar)

Cooked white rice, for serving (optional)

1. PREPARE THE FISH: Line a plate with paper towels and set near the stove. Pour ¾ inch oil into a large, deep, heavy-bottomed skillet and heat over medium-high heat until shimmering.

2. Season the fish with salt and pepper. Working in batches of two or whatever will comfortably fit in the pan, fry the fish skin-side down until the skin is crisped, 2 to 4 minutes. Flip and cook until the meat is just-cooked and flakes.

3. Drain the fish on the paper towels and transfer to a large platter or casserole dish.

4. MAKE THE MARINADE: In a nonreactive saucepan, combine the onions, carrots, bell pepper, chile, black peppercorns, allspice, thyme, and vinegar. Bring to a boil over medium heat. Reduce the heat and simmer until the onions have softened, 3 to 4 minutes. Pour this over the fish and allow to cool completely.

5. Serve at room temperature with rice (if desired). Or cover with plastic wrap and refrigerate overnight. It's even better the next day.

MOM'S FRIED CHICKEN

SERVES 2 TO 4

My mother could put a hurtin' on some fried chicken. She was a purist and used only a few ingredients to season the chicken, which was then fried in a black cast-iron skillet that had been her wedding present from my paternal grandmother. My parents married during the Great Depression and it was the only thing that my grandmother had to give. I still use it on very special occasions.

Fried chicken is a very interesting thing in the African American world. Chickens are thought to have originated in Asia, probably on the Indian subcontinent. They may be the first domesticated bird, and are almost certainly descendants of the dinosaurs. Once chickens were domesticated, they migrated from the subcontinent through the Middle East into the Mediterranean basin and from there to Europe. Some, though, feel that their journey to the New World may have taken a different route and that they may have arrived here with Polynesians before Columbus's voyages. No matter how they got here, they were taken to heart and stomach by all. African Americans were not left out.

2 cups rendered bacon fat, lard, or vegetable oil, for frying, plus more as needed

½ cup all-purpose flour

½ cup yellow cornmeal

1 tablespoon Bell's Seasoning (for poultry)

Kosher salt and freshly ground black pepper

1 whole chicken (3¼ to 4 pounds), cut into 8 pieces, patted dry

1. Line a wire rack with paper towels and set near the stove. In a large heavy cast-iron skillet, heat the fat to 325°F over medium-low heat. (Use a thermometer.) If you think all the chicken pieces won't fit in the skillet at once, cook in batches, but turn the oven on to the warm setting or to the lowest temperature possible to keep the chicken warm.

2. In a large brown paper bag or plastic food storage bag, combine the flour, cornmeal, Bell's Seasoning, and a few generous pinches of salt and pepper, as this will season the chicken. Add the chicken to the flour mixture a few pieces at a time. Shake well to ensure that each one is well coated and remove to a tray while you repeat with the rest of the chicken. Discard any remaining coating mixture in the bag.

3. Double-check the temperature of the oil and turn the heat up to medium-high. Arrange as many chicken pieces as will fit comfortably in the hot skillet without crowding and cook, turning occasionally, until all sides are golden brown, 15 to 20 minutes. If you're unsure of the doneness, use a thermometer—it should read 165°F in the center of a piece; however, for juicier chicken, you may safely remove chicken from the pan at 155°F in the center, as carryover cooking will continue to cook the chicken for a few minutes. If you don't have a thermometer, pierce the chicken to the bone with a small knife, if the juices run clear, the chicken is safe to eat.

4. Drain the cooked chicken for a minute or two on the paper towels. Adding more oil as needed, repeat with the remaining chicken if you are working in batches. Season the hot chicken with some more salt. Serve, or place in the oven to keep warm before serving.

GOSPEL BIRD

SERVES 4 TO 6

Named for its connection to Sunday dinner in many African American households and beyond, the Gospel bird is the plain roast chicken that often turned up on the family dinner table for the after-church meal. In my grandmother's house with ten children and occasional hungry parishioners, it had to go a long way.

The key to this recipe is seasoning the bird well, and the addition of an onion in the cavity, which slowly infuses the bird with its aroma. Tucking butter under the skin adds juiciness and promotes golden brown skin.

1 whole roasting chicken (3½ to 4 pounds), giblets removed

3 tablespoons cold unsalted butter

1 tablespoon fresh lemon juice

1 teaspoon sea salt

2 teaspoons Bell's Seasoning (for poultry)

½ teaspoon dried garlic slices (or garlic powder if unavailable)

1 teaspoon freshly ground black pepper

1 medium onion, peeled but whole

1. Preheat the oven to 450°F.

2. Place the chicken in a roasting pan and thoroughly pat dry with paper towels.

3. In a small saucepan, melt 2 tablespoons of the butter. Add the lemon juice and remove from the heat.

4. In a spice grinder, combine the salt, Bell's Seasoning, dried garlic, and pepper and pulse into a fine powder. Stir the spice blend into the lemon butter.

5. Cut the remaining 1 tablespoon butter into small bits. With your fingers, gently separate the chicken skin from the breast meat and distribute the butter bits under the skin.

6. Roll the onion in the seasoned butter and place it into the chicken's cavity. Rub the remaining seasoned butter all over the chicken.

7. Roast for 50 minutes. Check the chicken; the skin should be crisp and browned, and a thermometer inserted into the middle of the thigh should read 165°F. If not, roast for a few minutes more.

8. Let rest for a few minutes after coming out of the oven. Serve hot. (The onion may be removed, sliced, and served with the chicken.)

CHICKEN CROQUETTES

SERVES 4

Croquettes were a way of saving money, as the main ingredient could be stretched with bread crumbs, onion, celery, or other items. They were classics on the American table of the 1950s and probably hark back to my mother's days as a dietitian as much as to African American traditions. The most typical African American croquettes were made of salmon, prepared from canned salmon. These, made with cooked chicken, were considered fancier. Rather than breaded and fried as you might expect croquettes to be, these are something more akin to a seared chicken salad patty.

3 cups chopped cooked chicken (no skin; a rotisserie bird works well here)

½ cup minced celery

¼ cup minced Vidalia onion

¼ cup minced green bell pepper

2 large eggs

2 tablespoons heavy cream

½ teaspoon kosher salt

½ teaspoon freshly ground black pepper

4 tablespoons (½ stick) unsalted butter

1. In a medium bowl, mix together the chicken, celery, onion, and bell pepper.

2. In a small bowl, stir together the eggs and heavy cream. Fold it into the chicken and vegetables and season with the salt and pepper. The mixture will be thick. Form the mixture into 4 round patties 3 inches across.

3. In a heavy skillet, melt the butter over medium heat just until foamy. Add the croquettes and cook until golden brown on both sides, about 3 minutes per side. Serve hot.

BAKED HAM

SERVES 10 TO 12

Pigs are not native to the New World, and only arrived in this hemisphere with the Spaniards, but they have certainly been taken to the hearts and stomachs of almost all Americans. African Americans have traditionally delighted in bacon and in pork chops and desire to live "high on the hog," a figure of speech with a literal origin, meaning eating beyond pig's feet and offal and dining instead on the more prized cuts of the legs and loin. Baked Virginia hams were the summum bonum of Southern hospitality for many. Today, that is changing, but this recipe celebrates the ham. It may be considered a cheat to use a precooked ham, but this recipe yields wonderful results and the spicy peach/orange glaze that coats it has the sweetness of brown sugar and the bite of Dijon mustard.

1 (5-pound) bone-in fully cooked smoked ham

20 whole cloves, or more as needed

1½ pounds peaches, peeled (see Note), pitted, and cut into chunks, or frozen sliced peaches

1 cup freshly squeezed orange juice

¼ cup (packed) dark brown sugar

2 tablespoons Dijon mustard

1. Position an oven rack in the lowest slot and preheat the oven to 350°F. Line a large roasting pan with aluminum foil, or put a roasting rack in the pan.

2. Cut the skin off the ham with a sharp knife, score the ham fat into diamond shapes, and insert a clove in each diamond. Place in the pan (or on the rack).

3. In a food processor, pulse the peaches to form a thick puree. Add the orange juice, brown sugar, and mustard and pulse 5 more times, until smooth.

4. Use a pastry brush to coat the ham with half of the peach sauce. Reduce the oven temperature to 325°F. Bake the ham until the internal temperature is 140°F, about 2 hours.

5. Let the ham rest for 15 minutes. Slice from top bone to base and serve with the remaining peach sauce.

NOTE: To peel peaches, fill a large bowl with ice and water and set near the stove. Bring a pot of water to a boil over high heat. Add the peaches to the boiling water and blanch for 10 to 15 seconds, then remove them to the ice water. When cool enough to touch, peel the skins; they should slip off easily. If not, boil again for a few seconds.

DAD'S HARD-FRIED PORK CHOPS

SERVES 2 TO 3

While many savored smothered pork chops under rich gravy, at my home, my father liked them hard-fried and almost crisp. They were paired with vegetables and salads, but gravy was not really a part of things when they were served in our home: The star is the deep flavor of browned meat. Texturally these chops go against the contemporary preference for rosy-pink meat; in my experience the chewiness of these thin chops accentuates the flavor. I've had similar ones served with rice and beans at Haitian and Dominican restaurants.

½ cup all-purpose flour

½ cup fine-grind yellow cornmeal

Kosher salt and freshly ground black pepper

6 boneless loin pork chops (4 ounces each), ¼ inch thick, patted dry

6 tablespoons vegetable oil

1. Place a baking sheet in the oven and preheat to 200°F or its keep-warm setting.

2. In a medium brown paper bag or plastic food storage bag, add the flour and cornmeal and season well with salt and pepper. Season the pork chops also and add them, a few at a time, to the flour mixture. Shake well until they are coated with the mixture. (Discard any remaining coating mixture.)

3. In a heavy skillet, heat 3 tablespoons of the oil over medium-high heat until shimmering. Add 3 pork chops and cook until well browned on both sides, 2 to 3 minutes per side.

4. Transfer the cooked pork chops to the oven while you heat the remaining 3 tablespoons of oil in the skillet and cook the remaining pork chops. Serve hot.

OLD-FASHIONED PIG'S FEET

SERVES 4 TO 6

These are so simple but can be filling and comforting. As she aged, my mother would periodically prepare a meal of pig's feet with a hot potato salad. She delighted in sucking the skin, gristle, and meat from the bones. I once submitted a recipe for them to a publication and was given the notice that the dish was too basic. However, as with many foods like pig's feet, chicken feet, and bony parts that have sustained folks with less money for centuries, never underestimate the pleasure that can come from gnawing on rich meat, fat, and skin on the bone. Joy can be found when eating low on the hog as well.

6 to 8 whole pig's feet, split

2 bay leaves

6 black peppercorns, cracked

¼ cup cider vinegar

Kosher salt

Hot sauce, for serving

1. Using a sharp knife, scrape the pig's feet to remove any hair. (Recalcitrant hairs should be removed by singeing or by cutting off that piece of skin.)

2. In a stockpot, combine the pig's feet with enough water to cover. Bring to a boil over high heat and cook for 2 to 3 minutes.

3. Pour off the water along with any residue that accumulated on the surface. Rinse the feet and rinse out the pot. Return them to the pot and add fresh water to cover by about 5 inches. Add the bay leaves, peppercorns, and vinegar. Bring to a boil over high heat. Reduce the heat to a gentle, slowly bubbling simmer and cook for 1 hour.

4. Add salt to the water, enough so that it makes the liquid taste well-seasoned but not too salty. Continue cooking until the meat begins to fall off the bones, another 1½ hours.

5. Drain, discarding the bay leaves and peppercorns. Transfer the pig's feet to a platter and serve immediately with the hot sauce.

CHOUCROUTE GARNIE À MA MANIÈRE

SERVES 6 TO 8

It may seem strange to find a recipe for a French dish—a classic from Alsace, on the Franco-German border—in a cookbook that celebrates the food that is foundational to the cuisine of the United States. But, it also presents us as who we are now and what we eat now. Like most Black Americans, I have had a varied and complex relationship with the food of the world. While I eat, savor, and study the history of the food of Africans in the American diaspora, in daily life I am a culinary omnivore and I, like most African Americans, eat and enjoy the foods from all corners of the globe.

I find that many food writers of my generation either had culinary epiphanies in France or in Italy, whether they had particular connections to those cultures or were just swept up in the open love of food and drink in those societies—a far cry from that cultural norm in the mid-century United States. My own epiphany was in France, and I have been known to say that I suffer from galloping Francophilia. One of my favorite dishes is one that I first became acquainted with while studying in France. It is a sauerkraut stew that is rich with pork products and potatoes, the tang of the fermented cabbage rounded out by a long braise with smoked pork and sausages; a winter feast that is rustic in conception but utterly magnificent at the table. Decades ago, as a novice cook, I once served an exceedingly rudimentary version of choucroute, primarily using inexpensive supermarket hot dogs, to a very kind two-star Michelin chef who graciously ate it. This is a more accurate example of what it should be.

1¾ pounds meaty smoked ham hocks

8 ounces thick-sliced bacon, cut into 1-inch pieces

2 large onions, chopped

1 teaspoon juniper berries (or ½ cup gin)

1 teaspoon black peppercorns

10 whole cloves

8 allspice berries

3 bay leaves

32 ounces prepared sauerkraut (see Note), rinsed and squeezed dry

1 pound kielbasa, cut into serving-sized pieces

1 pound knockwurst, cut into serving-sized pieces

1 pound all-beef frankfurters, cut into ¼-inch pieces

2½ cups dry white wine

2 pounds small Yukon Gold potatoes, scrubbed well, cut into ½-inch pieces

Kosher salt

Variety of mustards, for serving

1. Preheat the oven to 350°F.

2. In a deep saucepan, combine the ham hocks and enough water to cover them by 4 inches. Bring to a boil over high heat. Reduce the heat to a slow simmer, cover, and cook until the meat is tender, about 2 hours, topping off with water occasionally as necessary.

3. Transfer the ham hocks to a medium bowl, reserving the broth in the pan. When the ham hocks are cool enough to handle, remove the meat from the bones. Discard the bones and reserve 2½ cups of the broth.

4. Heat a large heavy pot over medium-high heat. Add the bacon and cook until crisped, stirring as needed. Add the onions, juniper berries (if using gin, don't add it yet), peppercorns, cloves, allspice, and bay leaves to the pot. Cook until the onions are tender, about 5 minutes.

5. Add the sauerkraut, kielbasa, knockwurst, and frankfurters. Add the reserved broth and the wine (and the gin, if using). Bring to a boil and cook for 10 minutes. Reduce the heat to a slow simmer, cover, and braise until the sauerkraut is meltingly tender and you notice a developed flavor, 1 to 1½ hours.

6. Meanwhile, when you're about 20 minutes from finishing, cook the potatoes in a large pot of boiling salted water until tender.

7. To serve the choucroute, discard the bay leaves and arrange the sauerkraut, meats, and potatoes on a platter.

8. Serve hot, with the mustards.

NOTE: With all the rich ingredients, this dish can't help but be delicious, but the quality of the sauerkraut particularly matters. Try to find one that is naturally fermented, tangy but with real depth of flavor. It will make a big difference.

SIMPLE OKRA

SERVES 4

I am a passionate okra-vore. Whenever and however the mucilaginous pod is served, I say, "Yes, please," and lean in for more. I know that my love is true, because I never was forced to eat it as a child, as my mother could not abide it. I, however, like the sticky quality of the vegetable.

This preparation is the simplest rendering possible, and it doesn't particularly attenuate the texture of okra—though an acid, like vinegar or lemon, is used by some to cut down on the slip.

My love for okra—while it certainly does go back to my childhood—is also very much connected to my study of the foods of the African diaspora. I was thrilled when I learned many years ago that the plant may be native to the continent, and I have said that wherever okra points its green tip, Africa can be found. (Though, I admit, on the African continent I have come across some dishes where the sheets of exuded slipperiness have daunted even me.)

1 pound small young okra pods, trimmed

1 tablespoon fresh lemon juice

Kosher salt

Freshly ground black pepper

1. In a small saucepan, bring 2 cups water to a boil. Add the okra and simmer until the okra pods are fork-tender, about 3 minutes.

2. Remove from the heat, drain off the water, add the lemon juice, season well with salt and pepper, and toss to coat. Serve hot.

FRIED OKRA

SERVES 4

This is the way many prefer okra, as frying the pods takes away some of the slip. The bacon drippings used here are an essential flavoring to many African American fried dishes. They were usually held in a coffee can that sat on the back of the stove; cooks would pour rendered fat into the can, to be held for later use. Bacon fat's smoky savoriness gives the mild okra a delicious background flavor, and cornmeal gives a pleasant gritty crunch to the okra. For a photo, please see page 227.

1 pound small okra pods, trimmed

1 cup fine-grind yellow cornmeal

Kosher salt and freshly ground black pepper

½ cup rendered bacon fat or vegetable oil, for frying

1. Rinse the okra and cut it crosswise into ½-inch-thick pieces.

2. In a small brown paper bag or plastic food storage bag, combine the okra, cornmeal, and salt and pepper to taste. Shake to coat the okra evenly. (Discard any remaining coating mixture.)

3. Line a plate with paper towels and set near the stove. In a large cast-iron skillet, heat the bacon fat over medium-high heat until shimmering.

4. Working in batches to not crowd the pan, add the coated okra and spread out into a single layer. Cook until golden brown, 3 to 4 minutes. Flip the pieces to brown the other side, another 2 minutes.

5. Remove the okra with a slotted spoon and drain on the paper towels. Sprinkle with more salt and serve immediately.

OKRA FRITTERS

SERVES 6

Fritters were and are, in many African American households, the way to get another turn from leftovers or from fruits or vegetables that are a bit past their prime. Using the frying-in-deep-oil technique that connects Africans throughout the diaspora back to the continent, the fried tidbits can turn up at any point in the meal, from appetizer to dessert. These okra fritters could do double duty as an appetizer with a savory dipping sauce (such as the Tomato Chutney, page 237), but are equally at home as a vegetable side dish. Rather than chunks of okra encased in dough, the innovation here is that the okra is pulsed to become both the batter and the fritter, with a moist interior.

1 pound small okra pods, trimmed

½ teaspoon kosher salt, plus more to taste

½ teaspoon freshly ground black pepper

2 large eggs

2 teaspoons baking powder

¼ to ½ cup all-purpose flour

4 cups vegetable oil, or as needed

Hot sauce, for serving

1. In a medium saucepan, bring 1½ cups water to a boil over medium-high heat. Add the okra and cook until tender and easily smashed with a spoon, about 10 minutes.

2. Drain the okra and place it in a food processor. Pulse until you have a paste, 8 to 10 pulses.

3. Scrape the paste into a medium bowl and beat in the salt, pepper, eggs, baking powder, and enough flour to make a batter that resembles pancake batter.

4. Line a plate or baking sheet with paper towels and set near the stove. Pour 3 inches oil into a heavy saucepan or Dutch oven and heat the oil over medium-high heat to 375°F.

5. Working in batches to not crowd the pot, drop the batter into the oil by the tablespoonful and fry until golden brown, 3 to 4 minutes, turning the fritter once.

6. Drain the fritters on the paper towels and sprinkle with salt to taste. Serve immediately with hot sauce.

SUMMER SOUTHERN SUCCOTASH

SERVES 4 TO 6

The mixture of corn, lima beans, and tomatoes, stewed in their own juices, is a forgiving dish that can even be made from frozen ingredients in the middle of winter. It is at its best, though, at the end of summer when the ingredients are at their fresh-picked peak. In my version, I substitute African okra for the more traditional lima beans. While it's one of the African American South's most typical summer side dishes, its name comes from a traditional mix of corn, beans, and pumpkin called *sukquttahash* or *misickquatash* in the Narragansett language of what is now southern New England.

1 tablespoon vegetable oil or rendered bacon fat

2 medium Vidalia or other sweet onions, finely diced

1½ cups fresh corn kernels (from 2 ears of corn)

Kosher salt and freshly ground black pepper

4 small beefsteak tomatoes, peeled, seeded, and coarsely chopped

¼ pound small okra pods, trimmed and cut crosswise into ½-inch slices

1. In a heavy saucepan, heat the oil over medium heat until shimmering. Add the onions and corn kernels and sauté until the onions become translucent, 5 to 7 minutes. Season with a few pinches of salt and pepper.

2. Add the tomatoes, okra, and enough water to cover by 1 inch. Bring to a simmer. Season well with salt and pepper and cook over low heat, about 15 minutes, adding more water if necessary for a light, creamy consistency. Serve hot.

RUTABAGA PUREE

SERVES 4 TO 6

I am not sure how these northern European root vegetables became a part of my family's culinary tradition, but I know that they were on the table next to the mac and cheese and candied sweet potatoes every year at Thanksgiving, and I loved them so much that they would occasionally make other appearances at the family table. Their slightly smoky flavor comes from the addition of that African American culinary secret weapon . . . bacon. The pig, as it often does in traditional African American cooking, leaves a hint of flavor that is ineffable, but immediately recognizable. Here, it transforms the puree from a slurry of winter root vegetable into a complex medley of flavors: sweet, comforting, tangy, and bacon-y all at the same time.

6 thick-cut slices bacon, finely diced

2 pounds rutabaga, peeled and cut into 1-inch chunks

1 large russet potato, peeled and cut into 1-inch chunks

Pinch of sugar

Kosher salt and freshly ground black pepper

1. In a large heavy saucepan or Dutch oven, cook the bacon over medium heat until it begins to brown and its fat is rendered, about 4 minutes. Remove the bacon from the pan and set aside. Reserve the rendered fat in the pan.

2. Add the rutabaga, potato, and enough water to cover by 1 to 2 inches. Bring to a boil, reduce the heat to medium, and cook until the vegetables are tender and can be easily pierced with the tip of a paring knife, about 20 minutes.

3. In a colander set over a bowl, drain the vegetables, reserving the cooking liquid.

4. Transfer the vegetables to a bowl and use a potato masher to puree the vegetables until smooth, but not gluey. (Alternatively, use a ricer, or 8 to 10 pulses in a food processor.) Splash in some of the cooking water if needed to thin it out a little. Stir in the sugar and plenty of salt and pepper.

5. Transfer to a serving bowl and serve hot, topped with the cooked bacon.

TOMATO CHUTNEY

MAKES 3 CUPS

Putting up the harvest for the winter was an African American tradition: indeed an American tradition in areas where there are farms, and where bumper crops of vegetables have to be preserved so as not to go to waste. This savory chutney is a perfect way to use up slightly bruised summer-ripe tomatoes. I had many summers of making chutney on Martha's Vineyard; it was a hybrid dish that combined African American tradition and the summer bounty of the island. Sweet, tart, and spicy, the chutney can then be used to accompany everything from roasted chicken to fried fish.

12 Roma tomatoes, peeled and cut into slices

1-inch piece fresh ginger, peeled and grated

½ habanero chile, seeded (or ¼ chile, or less, if you are sensitive to spice)

2 large onions, peeled and quartered

2 garlic cloves, chopped

Leaves from 3 fresh basil sprigs

½ cup raisins

1 cup (packed) light brown sugar, plus more to taste

1 cup distilled white vinegar

Kosher salt

1. In a food processor, combine the tomatoes, ginger, habanero, onions, garlic, and basil. Pulse to form a thick, chunky puree.

2. In a heavy nonreactive saucepan, stir together the tomato mixture, raisins, brown sugar, vinegar, and a few pinches of salt. Bring to a boil over medium-high heat. Reduce the heat to a gentle simmer and continue to cook, stirring occasionally, until the chutney has a jam-like consistency, about 1½ hours. Keep an eye on it once the chutney starts to thicken; you will need to stir it more often from that point to prevent scorching.

3. Taste and add more salt or sugar if necessary. Pour or spoon into three sterilized ½-pint jars. The chutney can be served immediately but will keep, covered, in the refrigerator for up to 2 weeks.

WATERMELON RIND PICKLES

MAKES TWO 32-OUNCE JARS

"Waste not, want not" is a saying that applies in many American households, and finding innovative ways to use parts of items that might otherwise be discarded is a watchword in many families. It is surely from this frugality that the practice of pickling the white part of the watermelon rind developed. Far from the juicy sweetness of the red flesh, the rind provides more crunch and a natural tanginess accentuated by the brine. This pickle always managed to find its way into the relish dishes on my family's Thanksgiving table, and then rapidly disappeared.

Watermelon rind pickles have been in the African American culinary lexicon for more than a century; a version appears in *What Mrs. Fisher Knows about Old Southern Cooking*, published in 1881, the second known African American cookbook.

¼ cup Diamond Crystal kosher salt, or 2 tablespoons fine sea salt

3 cups cubed (1-inch) peeled watermelon rind (the white part, no green skin, some red flesh is okay)

½ cup cider vinegar

¼ cup balsamic vinegar

⅔ cup sugar

1 lemon, thinly sliced

2 (3-inch) cinnamon sticks, crushed

1 teaspoon whole cloves

1 teaspoon allspice berries

1. In a large bowl, whisk the salt into 8 cups of water to form a brine. Add the rinds and soak overnight.

2. Drain the rinds, rinse them with fresh water, and drain again.

3. Place the rinds in a large nonreactive saucepan, add 2 cups water, and simmer until fork-tender, 20 to 30 minutes.

4. In another large nonreactive saucepan, combine both vinegars, the sugar, lemon slices, cinnamon, cloves, and allspice. Bring to a boil. Reduce to a simmer and cook until a thin syrup forms, 12 to 15 minutes.

5. Drain the rinds, add them to the syrup, and continue to simmer until the rinds become translucent, 30 to 40 minutes.

6. Divide the rinds, lemon slices, and spices between two sterilized 32 ounce jars and add enough of the syrup to cover the rinds. The jars will not be completely full; there should be headspace. The pickles will keep in the refrigerator for 1 week.

WATERMELON

Watermelon is a tricky fruit in the United States. It is not tricky because it has difficulty growing or because it is different in taste. Rather, watermelon is tricky because it has a difficult history. For more than a century, African Americans, and our connection to this fruit that originated on the continent from which we hark, have been conjoined in images that demonize and diminish our humanity. Many of the particularly offensive images originated in the post-Reconstruction period, where it seemed to be a national necessity to demean and destroy any positive aspects of African American culture. You've likely seen these images—Black people depicted with exaggerated features, looking animalistic or monstrous, devouring massive wedges of watermelon.

But despite this, watermelons are indeed intimately connected with African Americans. The fruit originates in southern Africa, with the first watermelon harvest recorded in Ancient Egypt almost five thousand years ago. The fruit was introduced to Spain by the Moors, and Spaniards and enslaved Africans introduced it to the New World where it was recorded growing in Florida in the sixteenth century and in Massachusetts in the early seventeenth century.

Watermelon was especially prized in areas where the water supply was of uncertain purity or nonexistent, as the plant is 92 percent liquid and could quench thirst. This certainly meant survival for enslaved folk working in the hot sun.

The fruit also provided a means for creating income. In the South, Black farmers sold summer watermelon crops and in the North, women made extra income from pickling the rind, a part otherwise typically discarded. The pickles have been in the African American culinary lexicon for more than a century, and a version appears in *What Mrs. Fisher Knows about Old Southern Cooking*, the second known African American cookbook, published in 1881. In the twentieth century, Patsy Randolph, an African American entrepreneur, collected watermelon rinds from street vendors who sold individual slices and transformed them into pickles that she then sold. When I first moved to the Bedford-Stuyvesant neighborhood in Brooklyn, there was an enterprising gentleman who parked his car across the street from my house, opened his trunk, revealed a clutch of watermelons, and put up his sign "Watermelon, sweet like your woman!" I even call my summer place on Martha's Vineyard my Watermelon House, and delight in searching yard sales and antique shops for what a friend has dubbed "watermelonia" to decorate it.

South or North, summer-ripe or pickled, the fruit from Africa has become truly emblematic of hot July afternoons for all Americans, and the summer season brings out a host of self-proclaimed watermelon specialists who thump, prod, poke to select the sweetest, juiciest fruit to bring to picnics and barbecues for the delectation of all.

PICKLED PEACHES

MAKES 3 PINTS

Peaches are native to Asia and were probably first grown in China nearly four thousand years ago. None of that matters in this country, where peaches are found all over. While Georgia peaches are renowned, South Carolina likes to boast that they in fact produce more peaches than Georgia . . . and then Alabamans insist their Chilton County specimens are the finest.

Wherever you are, when they are ripe and there is a bumper crop of them, the best thing to do after you've eaten your fill and made ice cream is to pickle them and put them up so that they can be served with baked ham and pork chops throughout the winter. These would appear on my Virginia grandmother's table at Sunday dinner, in a crystal relish dish almost every time that we made the journey to dine. They are a celebration of the fruit and a serious nod to the tradition of pickling.

2 pounds firm but ripe peaches

2 cups (packed) light brown sugar

4 cups distilled white vinegar

½ teaspoon ground cinnamon

¼ teaspoon whole cloves

½ teaspoon ground allspice

¼ teaspoon freshly grated nutmeg

½ teaspoon finely grated lemon zest

1. Fill a large bowl with ice and water and set near the stove. Bring a pot of water to a boil over high heat. Add the peaches to the boiling water and cook for 10 to 15 seconds, then remove them to the ice water. When cool enough to touch, peel the skins; they should slip off easily. If not, boil again for a few seconds.

2. In a large nonreactive saucepan, combine the brown sugar and vinegar and bring to a boil over medium-high heat, stirring until the sugar has dissolved.

3. Meanwhile, pit the peaches and cut into wedges.

4. Add the peaches, cinnamon, cloves, allspice, nutmeg, and lemon zest to the vinegar mixture. Reduce the heat to medium-low and simmer until the peaches are tender, about 20 minutes.

5. If serving immediately, allow the pickled peaches to come to room temperature. Otherwise, spoon them into sterilized jars, top with the spiced vinegar, and let cool. The peaches will keep in the refrigerator for up to 2 weeks.

MISTER GOOD DADDY

SERVES 8

Our family friend Grayce Bayles was given to colorful outfits with accompanying hats. (Our affectionate family nickname for her was Big Bird.) She was teetotal. Interestingly enough, there is a thread of African American teetotalers alongside the alcohol-imbibing Saturday night sinners. I recently found my paternal grandmother's Temperance Pledge, and was more than happy that it had been tucked away and forgotten by most of my relatives. At any gathering where alcoholic drinks were being served to others, Mrs. Bayles would always request Mr. Good Daddy, her name for whatever nonalcoholic punch was available. This version is slightly fancier than the jazzed-up Kool-Aid that was the house wine for many an African American family.

1 (12-ounce) can frozen grape juice concentrate, thawed

1 (12-ounce) can frozen pink lemonade concentrate, thawed

1 liter ginger ale

Ice

1. In a large pitcher or punch bowl, stir together the grape juice and pink lemonade concentrates, ginger ale, and 2 cups water. Add ice and serve.

BLUFFS BLOODY

SERVES 1

The Bloody Mary is an American cocktail classic. I make mine with the special vodka that I prepare every summer when I arrive in the family cottage in Oak Bluffs, Massachusetts, by infusing what my liquor salesman calls "cost-effective vodka" with bell peppers and hot chiles. I start my mix when I arrive by pricking the peppers and chiles with a fork, then packing them into an iced tea jar with a spigot and pouring in the vodka. The number of bell peppers will depend on the size of the iced tea vessel. I find that a jalapeño or two and a habanero usually add enough zing, but it is a matter of taste. Pour in as much vodka as will fill the jar. After about 2 weeks, it's ready to go, infused with heat and, more important, the fruity-vegetal taste of peppers. It's my African American take on an American classic.

1 cup V8 Original 100% Juice

1 tablespoon fresh lemon juice

2 teaspoons Worcestershire sauce

Dash of hot sauce, or to taste

Pinch of celery salt

2 jiggers vodka (infused, if you'd like—see headnote)

Ice

1 scallion, trimmed, for garnish

1 pickled okra, for garnish

1 pepperoncini, for garnish (optional)

1. In a cocktail shaker, stir together the V8 juice, lemon juice, Worcestershire sauce, hot sauce, celery salt, and vodka until mixed well. Add ice and stir until chilled.

2. Pour into a large chilled stemmed glass. Garnish with the scallion, pepperoncini, and pickled okra.

BANANA FRITTERS

SERVES 4

When bananas were just about to go soft, black, and needed to be thrown out, that was the time to make banana fritters in my maternal grandmother's house. She, who had to feed a household consisting of her minister husband, ten children, and whatever parishioners dropped in, had to be creative with stretching the pastor's allowance. These tasty fritters could be prepared from bananas that were about to go, which she could purchase from the grocery store at a discount. They use a classic method of fritter making, in which cut-up pieces of banana are battered and then fried, producing a sweet, crisp, puffy, and rich treat.

Peanut oil, for frying

2 large eggs, lightly beaten

½ cup cold whole milk

3 tablespoons (packed) light brown sugar

1 cup all-purpose flour

⅛ teaspoon baking soda

4 ripe bananas, cut on the diagonal into 1-inch-thick slices

2 tablespoons powdered sugar, sifted

1. Line a baking sheet with paper towels and set near the stove. Pour 3 inches oil into a large heavy pot or deep fryer and heat to 375°F. (Use a thermometer.)

2. In a medium bowl, whisk together the eggs, milk, brown sugar, flour, and baking soda to form a smooth batter. Add the banana slices a few at a time, coating them well.

3. Using a long-handled slotted spoon, transfer a few coated slices at a time to the oil. Cook until nicely browned, 2 to 3 minutes, turning them once. Briefly drain on the paper towels and transfer the fritters to a platter.

4. Sprinkle with the powdered sugar and serve warm.

CRISP OATMEAL-ISH COOKIES

MAKES ABOUT 24 SMALL COOKIES

Cookies are an American way of life, from the ones sold by the Girl Scouts to those that are exchanged among friends at Christmastime, to those that are given for everything from Valentine's Day to get-well presents. Cookies are one of the foods that we have inherited from the Dutch, but are not often a big part of the African American dessert menu. We tend to prefer pies and cakes. These, though, are a variation on the ones that I baked with my mother in my childhood; she updated them from one of her dietitian school cookbooks and the crispy circles were a welcome after-school treat.

1 large egg

½ cup sugar

2 tablespoons unsalted butter, melted

⅔ cup old-fashioned rolled oats

3½ tablespoons sweetened dried coconut flakes, crushed with a rolling pin

2 tablespoons sliced almonds, crushed with a rolling pin

½ teaspoon kosher salt

¼ teaspoon vanilla extract

Dash of lemon extract

1. Preheat the oven to 325°F. Line a baking sheet with parchment paper or grease with cooking spray.

2. In a large bowl, lightly beat the egg. Gradually stir in the sugar until combined. Stir in the melted butter, oats, coconut, almonds, salt, vanilla and lemon extracts, making sure that they are well mixed.

3. Drop the mixture by heaping 1 tablespoon onto the prepared pan, spacing them 1½ inches apart. Dip a fork in cold water and use it to spread each portion into a round.

4. Bake until lightly browned, about 20 minutes, rotating the baking sheet front to back halfway through.

5. Cool completely on the baking sheet. Repeat to use all the dough and serve warm.

PEANUT BRITTLE

MAKES ABOUT 3 DOZEN SMALL PIECES

Recipes for peanut brittle, made with corn syrup and nuts, began appearing in American cookbooks in the nineteenth century, and rarely anywhere else. It is considered by many to be a truly American recipe.

Candies were often sold by enslaved and free African American women to raise a bit of extra cash. Hand-prepared candies were a tradition in my mother's family, with taffy pulls and peanut brittles being top on the list. This peanut brittle is certainly a simple candy to prepare; for many years I made it so often that I purchased a marble slab for cooling it.

2 cups sugar

¾ cup light corn syrup

2 cups unsalted dry-roasted peanuts

2 tablespoons unsalted butter, plus more for greasing

1 teaspoon baking soda

½ teaspoon vanilla extract

1. Line a baking sheet with parchment paper and lightly grease the paper with butter.

2. In a large saucepan, combine the sugar, ¼ cup water, and the corn syrup. Clip a candy thermometer to the side of the pan.

3. Cook over medium-high heat, stirring until the sugar has dissolved and the mixture starts to bubble and foam up, reaching 340°F.

4. Carefully use a heatproof spatula or spoon to stir in the peanuts until combined, making sure the temperature remains at 340°F. Remove the pan from the heat and stir in the butter, baking soda, and vanilla. Carefully transfer the mixture to the prepared baking sheet and quickly spread it out into an even layer.

5. Allow the peanut brittle to cool completely, 20 to 30 minutes. Once it has cooled and hardened, break it into pieces.

PEANUTS

Peanuts (*Arachis hypogaea*) are not nuts, but legumes or seed pods. They originated in the American Hemisphere (the Nahuatl name for "peanut" was *cacahuatl*, reflected to this day in the Spanish *cacahuate* and the French *cacahuète*) and were taken to the African continent early on by Portuguese and Spanish explorers and traders. There, they gradually supplanted the Bambara and Hausa groundnuts, other similar legumes, in popularity.

Most people think of the peanut in Africa simply as food, with thoughts of the rich peanut stew from Mali known as mafe, that may be at the origins of some of the United States' rich peanut soups. Often forgotten are the commercial implications of the peanut in places like nineteenth- and twentieth-century Senegal, when it was a major colonial cash crop. Massive amounts of them were produced and sent to France for use as cattle fodder and in the cooking oil industries.

On this side of the Atlantic, it was the Transatlantic Slave Trade and the enslaved Africans who returned peanuts to the northern part of the hemisphere in the 1700s. Then, they were used in crop rotation to replace valuable nutrients in the soil and as a convenient and nutritious snack. They would also become a culinary ingredient, and throughout the American Colonial period, peanut soups begin to appear on tables. The first known written recipe appears in Sarah Rutledge's 1847 cookbook, *The Carolina Housewife*. Her recipe for Groundnut Soup is simple:

> *To half a pint of shelled groundnuts well beaten up, add two teaspoons of flour and mix well. Put to them a pint of oysters and a pint and a half of water. While boiling, throw in a red pepper, or two, if small.*

Although the book attributes it to Rutledge, it is probably a version of a recipe that was originated by enslaved African cooks. Food scholars opine that the peanut soups that turn up in early Colonial cookbooks like that of Sarah Rutledge are Big House variations of more humble ones eaten by enslaved Africans. Indeed, in the hands of talented enslaved chefs, peanut soups became hallmarks of elegant Southern tables. One version is still served today in the tavern at Colonial Williamsburg. There are also a variety of peanut candies including the peanut patties that were sold on the streets of Charleston, South Carolina, under the name of "monkey meat."

The Civil War spread peanut usage to the northern and western United States, and the growth of traveling circuses transported snacking on them around the country. In the twentieth century, George Washington Carver found a multiplicity of uses for them, and their popularity continued to grow. Soon, the peanuts that sustained the enslaved became as much a part of American culture as hot dogs and baseball games.

PRALINES

MAKES 12 PIECES

These sweet treats are a candy from my adopted home of New Orleans. The combination of brown sugar and sweet pecans is a classic in the Crescent City on the Mississippi River. There, from the antebellum years up to the present moment, selling pralines has been a way for women of color to supplement incomes. It is still possible to find the candy sold out of car trunks under the name of pecan candy, as it is called by some folks. In the past, the sugary candy enabled some enslaved women to even purchase their freedom. While the recipe for La Colle (page 144) may be older, these pralines are included as a tribute to entrepreneurship of generations of African American women who have used food as a vehicle to make a way from no way. Pralines can be eaten as is, stored in tins to give as holiday gifts, or crumbled over vanilla ice cream for a New Orleans–style dessert.

1 cup (packed) light brown sugar
1 cup granulated sugar
½ cup light cream
2 tablespoons salted butter, plus more for greasing
1 cup pecan halves

1. Generously grease a large sheet of aluminum foil with butter or use a silicone mat and place it on a work surface.

2. In a heavy saucepan, combine both sugars and the cream. Clip a candy thermometer to the side of the pan. Bring the mixture to a boil over medium heat, stirring gently. Do not stir once the mixture has come to a boil.

3. When the mixture's temperature reaches 228°F on the thermometer, stir in the butter and pecans, and cook, stirring constantly, until the mixture reaches 236°F.

4. Remove from the heat and allow the mixture to cool for about 5 minutes. Using a wooden spoon, stir until the pecans are evenly coated but still glossy. Drop the praline mixture 1 tablespoon at a time onto the prepared foil or silicone mat, spacing them 1 inch apart. Make sure some pecans are in each praline.

5. Allow to cool thoroughly and serve.

HOT WATER GINGERBREAD

MAKES ONE 8-INCH PAN

This is not the gingerbread that is made into the gingerbread men and women that decorate holiday trees. Rather it is more like a gingery cake and antecedents of the recipe may date to the Middle Ages in Europe. It was a year-round favorite in my house, and it may also have its African American origin in plantation kitchens, where molasses was often the sweetener.

One day many years ago, when appearing on the late Dr. Betty Shabazz's radio show, I shared some with her and was delighted to hear her say that it had been a favorite of her husband's—she would make it for him often. I will now forever connect hot water gingerbread with Malcolm X.

Softened unsalted butter, for greasing

1 cup blackstrap molasses

½ cup boiling water

2¼ cups all-purpose flour

1 teaspoon baking soda

1½ teaspoons ground ginger

½ teaspoon ground cinnamon

½ teaspoon kosher salt

4 tablespoons (½ stick) unsalted butter, melted

¼ cup (packed) dark brown sugar

Whipped cream, for serving

1. Preheat the oven to 350°F. Use 1 tablespoon softened butter to grease an 8-inch square baking pan.

2. In a medium bowl, stir together the molasses and boiling water. Add the flour, baking soda, ginger, cinnamon, and salt, stirring to mix well. Add the melted butter and brown sugar, stirring to form a smooth batter. Pour into the pan.

3. Bake until a toothpick inserted in the center comes out clean, about 35 minutes.

4. Cut into 9 portions and serve warm or at room temperature. Serve the gingerbread topped with the whipped cream or served alongside.

APPLE PIE

MAKES ONE 9-INCH PIE

The adage "as American as apple pie" is often spouted by those who try to homogenize the country; it has never been so. Clearly, America is many things apart from the amber waves of grain that are evoked in the song, which came—along with apples—from Europe. Often, too, the hands that cooked the pies were of another color, and the land on which the pies were baked was usurped from still another group of people. And let's not forget that these pies are often seasoned with spices from Asia, the Caribbean, and beyond. The world is there in our American pie.

The more that we acknowledge that the history—both culinary and literal—of this country is the result of a similarly complex intertwining of cultures, the sooner we can, all of us, whatever our origins, come together around our bountiful communal table. And perhaps then we can all appreciate our good old-fashioned American apple pie to its fullest.

PIE DOUGH

- 2½ cups all-purpose flour, plus more for the work surface
- 1½ tablespoons granulated sugar
- 1 teaspoon kosher salt
- 6 tablespoons chilled vegetable shortening
- 14 tablespoons (1¾ sticks) chilled unsalted butter, cut into cubes
- 8 tablespoons ice water

FILLING

- 1 cup granulated sugar
- 2 tablespoons all-purpose flour
- 1 tablespoon grated lemon zest
- ¼ teaspoon ground allspice
- ¼ teaspoon ground cinnamon
- ¼ teaspoon freshly grated nutmeg
- ⅛ teaspoon kosher salt
- 1 tablespoon fresh lemon juice
- 2½ pounds McIntosh apples, peeled, cored, and cut into ½-inch slices
- 1 pound Granny Smith apples, peeled, cored, and cut into ½-inch slices

TO ASSEMBLE

- Egg wash: 1 large egg, lightly beaten
- 1 tablespoon turbinado sugar, for sprinkling

(recipe continues)

1. **MAKE THE PIE DOUGH:** In a food processor, pulse the flour, granulated sugar, and salt for about 5 seconds, until well combined. Add the shortening and pulse for about 10 seconds. Add the butter and pulse about 8 times, until it resembles coarse crumbs. Transfer to a large bowl.

2. Sprinkle in 5 tablespoons of the ice water. Using a spatula, stir and press the mixture together. Add more water, 1 tablespoon at a time if needed, until a dough forms.

3. Divide the dough in half and wrap each one in plastic wrap; forming disks about 4 inches wide. Refrigerate for up to 1 hour.

4. Before rolling the doughs, let them sit out for about 10 minutes, to soften slightly.

5. Lightly flour a work surface and rolling pin. Roll out the first disk of dough into a 12-inch round; loosely wrap the dough around the rolling pin and unroll onto a 9-inch pie plate, letting the excess dough hang over the edge.

6. Mold the dough into the pie plate by gently lifting the edge of the dough with one hand while pressing into the plate surface with the other hand. Cover with plastic wrap and refrigerate for about 20 minutes, until firm.

7. On the same floured surface, roll the second disk of dough into a 12-inch round and place on a parchment paper–lined baking sheet, cover, and refrigerate for up to 30 minutes.

8. Position an oven rack in the lower third of the oven and place a sheet pan on the rack. Preheat the oven to 500°F.

9. **MAKE THE FILLING:** In a large bowl, stir together the granulated sugar, flour, lemon zest, allspice, cinnamon, nutmeg, and salt. Add the lemon juice and apples and toss until evenly coated.

10. **TO ASSEMBLE:** Uncover the pie shell and add the apples with their juices, mounding them slightly in the center. Uncover the remaining refrigerated round of dough, wrap it loosely around the rolling pin, and gently unroll on top of the pie filling. Trim any overhang to about ½ inch beyond the rim of the pie plate and firmly pinch together the top and bottom crusts, tucking any overhang. Using your fingers, crimp evenly around the edges.

11. Cut four 3-inch slits on top, brush the surface with the egg wash, and sprinkle with the turbinado sugar.

12. Transfer to the heated sheet pan, reduce the oven temperature to 425°F, and bake for 25 minutes. Reduce the oven temperature to 375°F, rotate the sheet pan from front to back, and bake until golden brown and the juices are bubbling, 30 to 35 minutes longer.

13. Cool the pie on a wire rack to room temperature, 3 to 4 hours, before serving.

ACKNOWLEDGMENTS

It may take a village to raise a child, but it certainly takes a village to write a book. So, there are all of those who made-up my village to whom thanks and gratitude are due. First of all, to the generous friends and new acquaintances who allowed me time and who shared their stories and recipes with me: Julianne Vanderhoop, Renée Hunter, John Barbry, Sean Sherman, Melissa Guerra, Kit Bennett, Peter Rose, Lou Costa, Leni Sorensen, and Charlotte Lyons. My dear friend Abigail Rosen McGrath died before she could hold this book in her hand, and so I salute her memory.

Abundant thanks are also due to the police chief of my village: friend-become-editor Francis Lam, and the entire Clarkson Potter team, including associate editor Darian Keels, production editor Sohayla Farman, production manager Kim Tyner, designer Stephanie Huntwork, compositor Christina Self, marketer Stephanie Davis, and publicist David Hawk. The perceptive illustrations by Lisbeth Checo brought the contributors to life. And, there would be no book at all without the incredible photography of Kelly Marshall, the ministrations of recipe tester and food stylist extraordinaire Elle Simone Scott and her team, and fabulous prop stylist Jillian Knox, who built worlds within our studio walls.

Thanks are also due to the members of my team: my agent and sisterfriend Susan Ginsburg and her more than able assistant Catherine Bradshaw; my assistants Lily Smith and Noah Isabella Wiener; and to Jana Padula and Maya Majcen from the Harry Walker Agency.

I could not have made it through the horrors of COVID and its aftermath or the joys of a Netflix docuseries without my emotional support people. First among them: Pat Lawrence-Haughton and Noel Haughton, Linda Cohen, Yahdon Israel and Serenity, Kathy Belden and Will Holshouser, Mary Silsby, Mitzi Pratt and Flip Scipio, Lorin O. Lewis, Elaine Greenstein and Jose Medina, Cathy Young and Jim Cuddy, Nichole Green, Thom Jayne, Rick Ellis, Craig Samuel and Laura Samuel, Shoshana Guy, Philip Hoffman, Siddhartha Mitter, Eddie Garcia, Lionel Whiteman, JJ Cummings, Shan Wallace; neighbors the Payne-Hall and Levy families; cousins James Eliott Harris, Asantawaa Harris, and their families; Jocelyn Brown and family, and my new playmates at the New York Botanical Garden.

On Martha's Vineyard, where my work is usually finished, I owe thanks to David Amaral, Rhonda Conley, Barbara Phillips, Mark Anthony Chung, Eric Coles, Olive Tomlinson, Caroline Harris, Ryan Gussen, Dorria Ball, Robyn Bolles, Charlayne Hunter-Gault and the table sisterhood, Kahina Van Dyke, Gale Grain Monk, Glenn Roberts, and the Burnham Family.

In New Orleans, thanks are due to Kerry Moody; Mary Len Costa, Lenora Costa Stout, and family; Amanda McFillen, Patrick Dunne, Nathan Druse; Simon Gunning and Shelly Gunning; Michele Brierre, Gail McDonough Evans, Jim Evans, and Mar Paulsen.

My international family continues to support and sustain me, including Olive Allu and family, Gersoney Azevedo and family, my spiritual family at Casa Branca in Bahia, Roland Laval, the Bretteil family, Don Sloan, Jane Levi, Linda Swallow, Alain, and the Komaclo/Grimaud/Houemavo families.

As always, there is the one person that I have inadvertently forgotten. Please know that I am no less grateful for all that you did to sustain me. When I see you, I will add your name here: _____.

INDEX

Note: Page references in *italics* indicate recipe photographs.